R Deep Learning Pr

Master the techniques to design and develop neural network
models in R

Yuxi (Hayden) Liu
Pablo Maldonado

BIRMINGHAM - MUMBAI

R Deep Learning Projects

Commissioning Editor: Amey Varangaonkar
Acquisition Editor: Tushar Gupta
Content Development Editor: Aishwarya Pandere
Technical Editor: Prasad Ramesh
Copy Editor: Safis Editing
Project Coordinator: Nidhi Joshi
Proofreader: Safis Editing
Indexer: Pratik Shirodkar
Graphics: Tania Dutta
Production Coordinator: Shantanu Zagade

First published: February 2018

Production reference: 1160218

Published by Packt Publishing Ltd.
Livery Place
35 Livery Street
Birmingham
B3 2PB, UK.

ISBN 978-1-78847-840-3

www.packtpub.com

`mapt.io`

Mapt is an online digital library that gives you full access to over 5,000 books and videos, as well as industry leading tools to help you plan your personal development and advance your career. For more information, please visit our website.

Why subscribe?

- Spend less time learning and more time coding with practical eBooks and Videos from over 4,000 industry professionals

- Improve your learning with Skill Plans built especially for you

- Get a free eBook or video every month

- Mapt is fully searchable

- Copy and paste, print, and bookmark content

PacktPub.com

Did you know that Packt offers eBook versions of every book published, with PDF and ePub files available? You can upgrade to the eBook version at `www.PacktPub.com` and as a print book customer, you are entitled to a discount on the eBook copy. Get in touch with us at `service@packtpub.com` for more details.

At `www.PacktPub.com`, you can also read a collection of free technical articles, sign up for a range of free newsletters, and receive exclusive discounts and offers on Packt books and eBooks.

Contributors

About the authors

Yuxi (Hayden) Liu is currently an applied research scientist focused on developing machine learning models and systems for given learning tasks. He has worked for a few years as a data scientist, and applied his machine learning expertise in computational advertising. He earned his degree from the University of Toronto, and published five first-authored IEEE transaction and conference papers during his research. His first book, titled *Python Machine Learning By Example*, was ranked the #1 bestseller in Amazon India in 2017. He is also a machine learning education enthusiast.

Pablo Maldonado is an applied mathematician and data scientist with a taste for software development since his days of programming BASIC on a Tandy 1000. As an academic and business consultant, he spends a great deal of his time building applied artificial intelligence solutions for text analytics, sensor and transactional data, and reinforcement learning. Pablo earned his PhD in applied mathematics (with focus on mathematical game theory) at the Universite Pierre et Marie Curie in Paris, France.

This book would not have been possible without the continuous feedback from my students from lectures and seminars in Mexico, Czech Republic, and Ukraine. Teaching has taught me a great deal!

About the reviewer

Davor Lozić is an engineer who works mostly on software architecture and distributed systems. He found R by doing a lot of fun predictions with data from distributed systems and user events, and continues using it for statistical modeling. He is also a professor at the University of Zagreb, where he teaches software architecture and distributed database systems. Davor, along with his cat, Dora, is working on technical reviews of Packt books and is happy with every new release.

Packt is searching for authors like you

If you're interested in becoming an author for Packt, please visit authors.packtpub.com and apply today. We have worked with thousands of developers and tech professionals, just like you, to help them share their insight with the global tech community. You can make a general application, apply for a specific hot topic that we are recruiting an author for, or submit your own idea.

Table of Contents

Preface

In this book, we have tried to make a case for using deep learning within R. Most deep learning power-users would shun R and go for other languages, such as Python. We, however, believe that R has a solid ecosystem of packages, and visualization and manipulation tools, that can be combined with deep learning libraries to create interesting projects. R also has a huge base of users without a software engineering background (perhaps you are one of them?), and those users are increasingly interested in applications that deep learning is making possible, but they do not have time to learn Python.

Who this book is for

This book is meant mainly for two types of readers: professionals who use R in their daily work and want to know some of the tricks and best practices that we have discovered in our projects, and anyone who wants to jump into the field of deep learning with concrete use cases in mind. This is not a tutorial in R or machine learning; it is rather a real-world showcase of how deep learning can be used in industry, with examples borrowed from our own experience.

What this book covers

Chapter 1, *Handwritten Digit Recognition Using Convolutional Neural Networks*, is where we start working on the first project of the book. We will begin with a recap of logistic regression and multilayer perceptron. We'll solve the problem with these two algorithms. We will then move on to the biologically inspired variants of multilayer perceptron—convolutional neural networks (CNNs). We will also cover the basics and core concepts of deep learning.

Chapter 2, *Traffic Sign Recognition for Intelligent Vehicles*, explains how to use CNNs for another application—traffic sign detection. We will also cover several important concepts of deep learning in this chapter and get readers familiar with other popular frameworks and libraries, such as Keras and TensorFlow. We will also introduce the dropout technique as a regularization approach and utilize data augmentation techniques to deal with a lack of training data.

Chapter 3, *Fraud Detection with Autoencoders*, introduces a type of deep learning model that can be used for anomaly detection. Outliers can be found within a collection of images, a text corpus, or transactional data. We will dive into applications of autoencoders and how they can be used for outlier detection in this domain.

Chapter 4, *Text Generation Using Recurrent Neural Networks*, introduces different models of neural networks that try to capture the elusive properties of memory and abstraction to produce powerful models. We will apply different methods to tackle the text generation problem and suggest directions of further exploration.

Chapter 5, *Sentiment Analysis with Word Embeddings*, shows how to use the popular GloVe algorithm for sentiment analysis, as well as other, less abstract tools. Although this algorithm is, strictly speaking, not a deep learning application, it belongs to the modern (as of 2018) toolkit of the data scientist, and it can be combined with other deep learning techniques.

To get the most out of this book

You should be comfortable with R and RStudio and have some knowledge of college-level mathematics (calculus and linear algebra). Working knowledge of basic machine learning algorithms for classification, regression problems, and clustering might be helpful, but it is not strictly required.

Download the example code files

You can download the example code files for this book from your account at www.packtpub.com. If you purchased this book elsewhere, you can visit www.packtpub.com/support and register to have the files emailed directly to you.

You can download the code files by following these steps:

1. Log in or register at www.packtpub.com.
2. Select the **SUPPORT** tab.
3. Click on **Code Downloads & Errata**.
4. Enter the name of the book in the **Search** box and follow the onscreen instructions.

Once the file is downloaded, please make sure that you unzip or extract the folder using the latest version of:

- WinRAR/7-Zip for Windows
- Zipeg/iZip/UnRarX for Mac
- 7-Zip/PeaZip for Linux

The code bundle for the book is also hosted on GitHub at `https://github.com/PacktPublishing/R-Deep-Learning-Projects`. We also have other code bundles from our rich catalog of books and videos available at `https://github.com/PacktPublishing/`. Check them out!

Conventions used

There are a number of text conventions used throughout this book.

`CodeInText`: Indicates code words in text, database table names, folder names, filenames, file extensions, pathnames, dummy URLs, user input, and Twitter handles. Here is an example: "Similarly, for the second sample, `(a "0")`, we run:"

A block of code is set as follows:

```
> for (i in 1:16) {
+ outputData <- as.array
(executor$ref.outputs$activation15_output)[,,i,1]
+ image(outputData, xaxt='n', yaxt='n',
col=grey.colors(255)
+ )
+ }
```

When we wish to draw your attention to a particular part of a code block, the relevant lines or items are set in bold:

```
library(R6)
logit <- function(x){
 1/(1+exp(-x))
}
```

Bold: Indicates a new term, an important word, or words that you see onscreen. For example, words in menus or dialog boxes appear in the text like this. Here is an example: "Once logged in, click on **Create New App**."

 Warnings or important notes appear like this.

 Tips and tricks appear like this.

Get in touch

Feedback from our readers is always welcome.

General feedback: Email `feedback@packtpub.com` and mention the book title in the subject of your message. If you have questions about any aspect of this book, please email us at `questions@packtpub.com`.

Errata: Although we have taken every care to ensure the accuracy of our content, mistakes do happen. If you have found a mistake in this book, we would be grateful if you would report this to us. Please visit `www.packtpub.com/submit-errata`, selecting your book, clicking on the Errata Submission Form link, and entering the details.

Piracy: If you come across any illegal copies of our works in any form on the Internet, we would be grateful if you would provide us with the location address or website name. Please contact us at `copyright@packtpub.com` with a link to the material.

If you are interested in becoming an author: If there is a topic that you have expertise in and you are interested in either writing or contributing to a book, please visit `authors.packtpub.com`.

Reviews

Please leave a review. Once you have read and used this book, why not leave a review on the site that you purchased it from? Potential readers can then see and use your unbiased opinion to make purchase decisions, we at Packt can understand what you think about our products, and our authors can see your feedback on their book. Thank you!

For more information about Packt, please visit `packtpub.com`.

1
Handwritten Digit Recognition Using Convolutional Neural Networks

We kick off our R deep learning journey with the fundamental and core concepts of deep learning, and a deep learning 101 project—handwritten digit recognition. We will start with what deep learning is about, why we need it, and its evolution in recent years. We will also discuss why deep learning stands out and several typical deep learning applications. With the important deep learning concepts in mind, we get it started with our image classification project where we first conduct exploratory analysis on the data and make an initial attempt using shallow single-layer neural networks. Then we move on with deeper neural networks and achieve better results. However, we argue that chaining more hidden layers does not necessarily improve classification performance. The key is to extract richer representation and more informative features. And **convolutional neural networks (CNNs)** are the way to go! We will be demonstrating how we boost the digit recognition accuracy to nearly 99% with CNNs, which are well suited to exploiting strong and unique features that differentiate between images. We finally wrap up the chapter after several more experiments and validations.

We will look into these topics in detail:

- What is deep learning and what is special about it
- Applications of deep learning
- Exploratory analysis on MNIST handwritten digit data
- Handwritten digit recognition using logistic regression and single-layer neural networks with the `nnet` package
- Handwritten digit recognition using deep neural networks with the `MXNet` package
- Rectified linear unit
- The mechanics and structure of convolutional neural networks
- Handwritten digit recognition using convolutional neural networks with the `MXNet` package
- Visualization of outputs of convolutional layers
- Early stopping in deep neural networks

What is deep learning and why do we need it?

Deep learning is an emerging subfield of machine learning. It employs **artificial neural network (ANN)** algorithms to process data, derive patterns or to develop abstractions, simulating the thinking process of a biological brain. And those ANNs usually contain more than one **hidden layer**, which is how deep learning got its name—machine learning with *stacked* neural networks. Going beyond shallow ANNs (usually with only one hidden layer), a deep learning model with the right architectures and parameters can better represent complex non-linear relationships.

Here is an example of a shallow ANN:

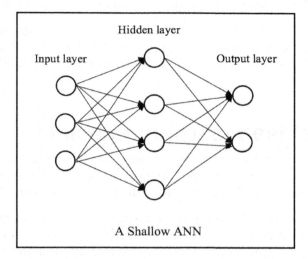

A Shallow ANN

And an example of a deep learning model:

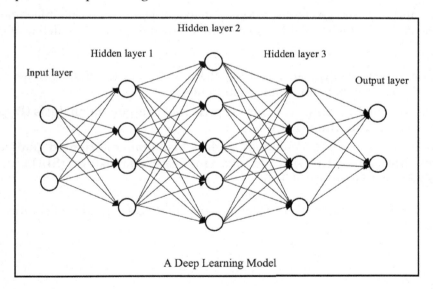

A Deep Learning Model

Don't feel scared, regardless of how complicated it might sound or look. We will be going from shallow to deep dives into deep learning throughout five projects in this book.

First of all, as a part of the broad family of machine learning, deep learning can be used in supervised learning, semi-supervised learning, as well as unsupervised learning tasks, even reinforcement learning tasks. So what sets it apart from traditional machine learning algorithms?

What makes deep learning special?

Deep learning employs a stack of multiple hidden layers of non-linear processing units. The input of a hidden layer is the output of its previous layer. This can be easily observed from the examples of a shallow neural network and a deep neural network shown previously.

Features are extracted from each hidden layer. Features from different layers represent abstracts or patterns of different levels. Hence, higher-level features are derived from lower-level features, which are extracted from previous layers. All these together form a hierarchical representation learned from the data.

Take the cats and dogs image classification as an example, in traditional machine learning solutions, the classification step follows a feature extraction process, which is often based on:

- Domain knowledge, such as color, shape, color of the animals, shape of the ears in this case, which are usually hand-crafted
- Dimensionality reduction, such as **principal component analysis (PCA)**, **Latent Dirichlet Allocation (LDA)**
- Feature engineering techniques, such as **histogram of oriented gradients transformation (HOG)**, **Scale Invariant Feature Transform (SIFT)**, and **Speeded up Robust Features (SURF)**

The workflow of traditional machine learning solution to cats and dogs classification is displayed as follows:

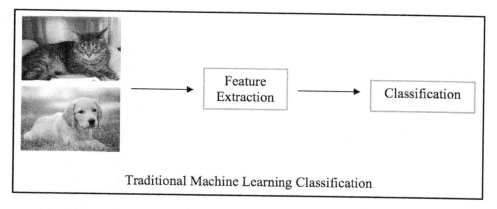

Traditional Machine Learning Classification

However, in deep learning based solutions (such as CNNs, which we will be learning shortly), hierarchical representations are derived throughout the latent learning process and features of the highest level are then fed into the final classification step. These features capture the important and distinguishable details in the cat and dog images. Depending on the magic worked in hidden layers:

- The low-level features can be edges, lines or dots of whiskers, nose or eyes, ears and so on
- The higher-level features can be outlines or contours of the animals

The entire workflow of deep learning solution is shown as follows:

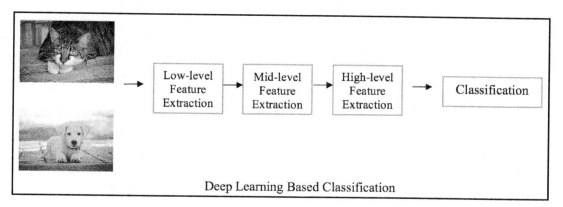

Deep Learning Based Classification

Deep learning removes those manual or explicit feature extraction steps, and instead relies on the training process to automatically discover useful patterns underneath the input data. And through tweaking the layout (number of layers, number of hidden units for a layer, activation function, and so on) of the networks, we can find the most efficient sets of features.

Recall the example of the shallow ANN and that of the deep learning model in the last section, data flow one-way from the input layer to the output. Besides feedforward architectures, deep learning models allow data to proceed in any direction, even to circle back to the input layer. Data looping back from the previous output becomes part of the next input data. **Recurrent neural networks (RNNs)** are great examples. We will be working on projects using RNNs later in this book. For now, we can still get a sense of what the recurrent or cycle-like architecture looks like from the diagram of RNNs as follows:

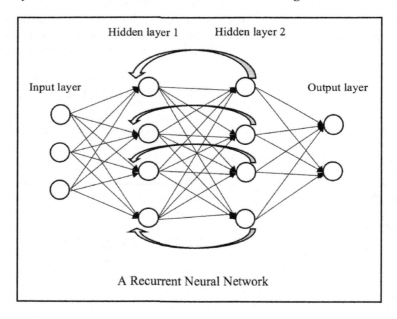

A Recurrent Neural Network

The recurrent architecture makes the models applicable to time series data and sequences of inputs. As data from previous time points goes into the training of the current time point, the deep learning recurrent model effectively solves a time series or sequence learning problem in a feedforward manner. In traditional machine learning solutions (read more in *Machine Learning for Sequential Data: A Review* by T. Dietterich) to time series problems, sliding windows of previous lags are usually provided as current inputs. This can be ineffective as the size of the sliding windows needs to be decided and so does the number of windows, while the recurrent models figure out timely or sequential relationships themselves.

Although we are discussing here all the advantages about deep learning over the other machine learning techniques, we did not make any claim or statement that the *modern* deep learning is superior to the *traditional* machine learning. That's right, there is *no free lunch* in this field, which was also emphasized in my last book, *Python Machine Learning By Example*. There is no single algorithm that can solve all machine learning problems more efficiently than others. It all depends on specific use cases - in some applications, the "traditional" ones are a better fit, or a deep learning setting makes no difference; in some cases, the "modern" ones yield better performance.

Next, we will see some typical applications of deep learning that will better motivate us to get started in deep learning projects.

What are the applications of deep learning?

Computer vision and image recognition is often considered the first area where breakthroughs of deep learning occurred. Handwritten digit recognition has become a Hello World in this field, and a common evaluation set for image classification algorithms and techniques is the scanned document dataset constructed from the **National Institute of Standards and Technology** (**NIST**), called **MNIST** (**M** stands for **modified**, which means data is pre-processed for the ease of machine learning processes).

Some examples from MNIST are shown as follows:

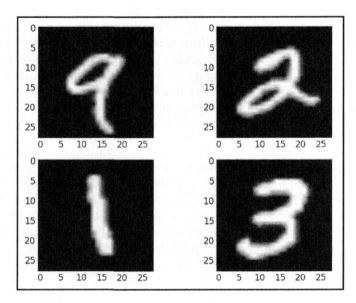

Some researchers have so far achieved the best performance 0.21% error rate on the MNIST dataset using CNNs. Details can be found in the paper, *Regularization of Neural Networks using DropConnect,* published in the **International Conference on Machine Learning (ICML)** in 2013. Other comparable results, for example 0.23%, 0.27% and 0.31%, are also yielded by CNNs and deep neural networks. However, traditional machine learning algorithms with sophisticated feature engineering techniques could only yield error rates ranging from 0.52% to 7.6%, which were achieved by using **Support Vector Machine (SVMs)** and pairwise linear classifiers respectively.

Besides image recognition (such as the well known face recognition), the applications of deep learning are extended to more challenging tasks including:

- Image-based search engines, which cover image classification and image similarity encoding, heavily utilizing deep learning techniques.
- Machine vision, with self-driving cars as an example, which interprets 360° camera views to make decisions in real time.

- Color restoration from black and white photos—the examples after color recovery from `http://hi.cs.waseda.ac.jp/~iizuka/projects/colorization/extra.html` are impressive.
- Image generation, including handwriting, cat images, and even video game images, or whatever image you name it. For example, we use an interesting playground, `https://www.cs.toronto.edu/~graves/handwriting.html` (developed by Alex Graves from the University of Toronto), to create handwritings of the title of this book in three different styles:

Natural language processing (NLP) is another field where deep learning is dominant in modern solutions. Recall we described deep learning models with recurrent architecture are appropriate for sequences of inputs, such as natural language and text. In recent years, deep learning has greatly helped to improve:

- Machine translation, for example the sentence-based **Google Neural Machine Translation system** (**GNMT**) which utilizes deep RNNs to improve accuracy and fluency
- Sentiment analysis, information retrieval, theme detection and many other common NLP applications, where deep learning models have achieved state-of-the-art performance thanks to word embedding techniques
- Text generation, where RNNs learn the intricate relationship between words (including punctuation) in sentences and to *write* text, to become an author or a virtual Shakespeare

Image captioning generation, also known as image to text, couples recent breakthroughs in computer vision and NLP. It leverages CNNs to detect and classify objects in images, and assigns labels to those objects. It then applies RNNs to describe those labels in a comprehensible sentence. The following examples are captured from the web demo from http://cs.stanford.edu/people/karpathy/deepimagesent/generationdemo/ (developed by Andrej Karpathy from Stanford University):

a train is traveling down the tracks near a building

a train traveling down tracks next to a forest

Similarly, sound and speech is also a field of sequential learning, where machine learning algorithms are applied to predict time series or label sequence data. Speech recognition has been greatly revolutionized by deep learning. And now, deep learning based products like Apple's Siri, Amazon's Alexa, Google Home, Skype Translator and many others are "invading" our lives, in a good way for sure. Besides an author writing text, deep learning models can also be a music composer. For example, Francesco Marchesani from the Polytechnic University of Milan was able to train RNNs to produce Chopin's music.

Additionally, deep learning also excels in many use cases in video. It makes significant contributions to the boost of virtual reality with its capability of accurate motion detection, and to the advance of real-time behavior analysis in surveillance videos. Scientists from Google, DeepMind, and Oxford even built a computer lip reader called LipNet, achieving a success rate of 93%.

Besides supervised and unsupervised learning cases, deep learning is heavily used in reinforcement learning. Robots who can handle objects, climb stairs, operate in kitchens are not new to us. Recently, Google's AlphaGo beating the world's elite *Go* players received widespread media coverage. Nowadays, everybody looks forward to seeing self-driving cars being out in the market in just one or two years. These have all benefited from the advance of deep learning in reinforcement learning. Oh, and don't forget computers are taught to play the game, FlappyBird!

We did not even mention bioinformatics, drug discovery, recommendation systems in e-commerce, finance, especially the stock market, insurance and the **Internet of Things (IoT)**. In fact, the list of deep learning applications is already long, and only gets longer and longer.

I hope this section excited you about deep learning and its power of providing better solutions to many machine learning problems we are facing. Artificial intelligence has a brighter future thanks to the advance of deep learning.

So what are we waiting for? Let's get started with handwritten digit recognition!

Handwritten digit recognition using CNNs

For sure, we begin with exploration of the handwritten digit dataset.

Get started with exploring MNIST

The MNIST dataset from `http://yann.lecun.com/exdb/mnist/` consists of a training set of 60,000 samples, and a testing set of 10,000 samples. As said previously, images were originally taken from the NIST, and then centered and resized to the same height and width (28 * 28).

Rather than handling the `ubyte` files, `train-images-idx3-ubyte.gz` and `train-labels-idx1-ubyte.gz` in the preceding website and merge them, we use a dataset that is well-formatted from the Kaggle competition Digit Recognizer, `https://www.kaggle.com/c/digit-recognizer/`. We can download the training dataset, `train.csv` directly from `https://www.kaggle.com/c/digit-recognizer/data`. It is the only labeled dataset provided in the site, and we will use it to train classification models, evaluate models and do predictions. Now let's load it up:

```
> data <- read.csv ("train.csv")
> dim(data)
[1] 42000 785
```

We have 42,000 labeled samples available, and each sample has 784 features, which means each digit image has 784 (28 * 28) pixels. Take a look at the label and the first 5 features (pixels) for each of the first 6 data samples:

```
> head(data[1:6])
label pixel0 pixel1 pixel2 pixel3 pixel4
1 1 0 0 0 0 0
2 0 0 0 0 0 0
3 1 0 0 0 0 0
4 4 0 0 0 0 0
5 0 0 0 0 0 0
6 0 0 0 0 0 0
```

The target label ranging from 0 to 9 denotes 10 digits:

```
> unique(unlist(data[1]))
[1] 1 0 4 7 3 5 8 9 2 6
```

The pixel variable ranges from 0 to 255, representing the brightness of the pixel, for example 0 means black and 255 stands for white:

```
> min(data[2:785])
[1] 0
> max(data[2:785])
[1] 255
```

Now let's take a look at two samples, first, the fourth image:

```
> sample_4 <- matrix(as.numeric(data[4,-1]), nrow = 28, byrow = TRUE)
> image(sample_4, col = grey.colors(255))
```

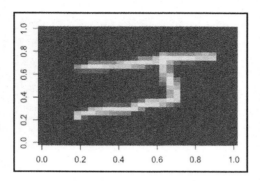

Where we reshaped the feature vector of length 784 into a matrix of 28 * 28.

Second, the 7th image:

```
> sample_7 <- matrix(as.numeric(data[7,-1]), nrow = 28, byrow = TRUE)
> image(sample_7, col = grey.colors(255))
```

The result is as follows:

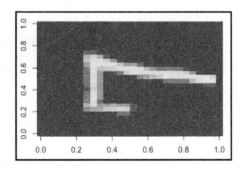

We noticed that the images are rotated 90 degrees to the left. To better view the images, a rotation of 90 degrees clockwise is required. We simply need to reserve elements in each column of an image matrix:

```
> # Rotate the matrix by reversing elements in each column
> rotate <- function(x) t(apply(x, 2, rev))
```

Now visualize the rotated images:

```
> image(rotate(sample_4), col = grey.colors(255))
```

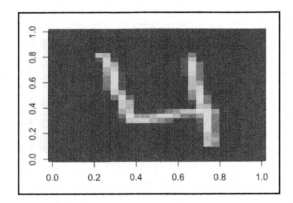

```
> image(rotate(sample_7), col = grey.colors(255))
```

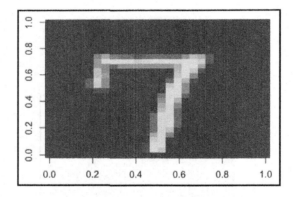

After viewing what the data and images behind look like, we do more exploratory analysis on the labels and features. Firstly, because it is a classification problem, we inspect whether the classes from the data are balanced or unbalanced as a good practice. But before doing so, we should transform the label from integer to factor:

```
> # Transform target variable "label" from integer to factor, in order to
perform classification
> is.factor(data$label)
[1] FALSE
> data$label <- as.factor(data$label)
> is.factor(data$label)
[1] TRUE
```

Now, we can summarize the label distribution in counts:

```
> summary(data$label)
0  1  2  3  4  5  6  7  8  9
4132  4684  4177  4351  4072  3795  4137  4401  4063  4188
```

Or combined with proportion (%):

```
> proportion <- prop.table(table(data$label)) * 100
> cbind(count=table(data$label), proportion=proportion)
count proportion
0  4132  9.838095
1  4684  11.152381
2  4177  9.945238
3  4351  10.359524
4  4072  9.695238
5  3795  9.035714
6  4137  9.850000
7  4401  10.478571
8  4063  9.673810
9  4188  9.971429
```

Classes are balanced.

Now, we explore the distribution of features, the pixels. As an example, we take the 4 pixels from the central 2*2 block (that is, `pixel376`, `pixel377`, `pixel404`, and `pixel405`) in each image and display the histogram for each of the 9 digits:

```
> central_block <- c("pixel376", "pixel377", "pixel404", "pixel405")
> par(mfrow=c(2, 2))
> for(i in 1:9) {
+ hist(c(as.matrix(data[data$label==i, central_block])),
+ main=sprintf("Histogram for digit %d", i),
+ xlab="Pixel value")
+ }
```

The resulting pixel brightness histograms for digit 1 to 4 are displayed respectively, as follows:

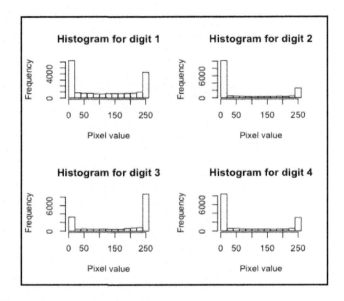

Histograms for digits 5 to 9:

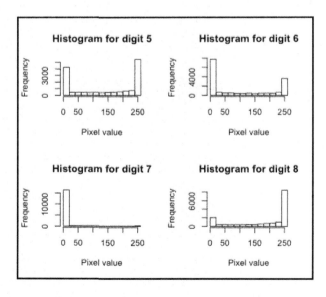

And that for digit 9:

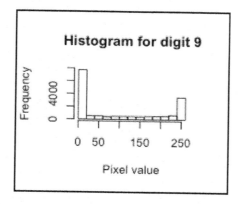

The brightness of central pixels is distributed differently among 9 digits. For instance, the majority of the central pixels are bright, as digit 8 is usually written in a way that strokes go through the center; while digit 7 is not written in this way, hence most of the central pixels are dark. Pixels taken from other positions can also be distinctly distributed among different digits.

The exploratory analysis we just conducted helps move us forward with building classification models based on pixels.

First attempt – logistic regression

We start off with probably the most basic classifier, the logistic regression, to be specific multinomial logistic regression as it is a multiclass case. It is a probabilistic linear classifier parameterized by a weight matrix *W* (also called coefficient matrix) and a bias (also called intercept) vector *b*. And it maps an input vector *x* to a set of probabilities $P(y=1)$, $P(y=2)$,..., $P(y-K)$ for *K* possible classes.

A multinomial logistic regression for two possible classes can be represented graphically as follows:

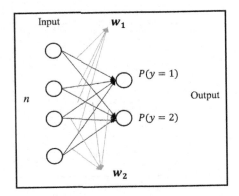

Suppose x is n-dimension, then the weight matrix W is of size n by K with each column W_k representing the coefficients associated with class k; similarly, the bias vector b is of length K, with each element b_k served as the bias for class k. For simplicity, the bias b can be viewed as an additional row in the weight matrix W. So the probability of x being class k can be expressed mathematically as:

$$P(y = k|x, W) = softmax_k(Wx)$$

$$= \frac{exp(w_k x)}{\sum_{j=1}^{j=k} exp(w_j x)}$$

Where *softmax()* denotes the softmax function and that is why multinomial logistic regression is often called softmax regression.

Given a set of training samples $(x^{(1)}, y^{(1)}), (x^{(2)}, y^{(2)}), \ldots (x^{(i)}, y^{(i)}) \ldots, (x^{(m)}, y^{(m)})$ where $y \in 1, 2, \ldots, K$, the optimal model w is obtained by minimizing the cost (also called log loss), which is defined as:

$$J(W) = - \left[\sum_{i=1}^{m} \sum_{k=1}^{k} 1\{y^{(i)} = k\} log \frac{exp(w_k x)}{\sum_{j=1}^{j=k} exp(w_j x)} \right]$$

$$\text{where} \quad 1\{y^{(i)} = k\} = \begin{cases} 1, & if \ y^{(i)} = k \\ 0, & otherwise \end{cases}$$

As usual we resort to gradient descent, an iterative optimization algorithm, to solve for the optimal w. In each iteration, w moves a step that is proportional to the negative derivative Δw of the objective function at the current point. That is, $w := w - \eta \Delta w$, where η is the learning rate. Each column Δw_k of Δw can be computed as:

$$\triangle w_k = \frac{\partial}{\partial w_j} J(w) = -\sum_{i=1}^{m} [x^{(i)}(1\{y^{(i)} = k\} - P(y^{(i)} = k \mid x^{(i)}, W))]$$

The well trained model, the optimal w will be used to classify a new sample x' by:

$$y' = \underset{k}{\text{argmax}} \frac{\exp\left(w_k x'\right)}{\sum_{j=1}^{j=K} \exp\left(w_j x'\right)} = \underset{k}{\text{argmax}} \left(w_k x'\right)$$

Armed with the mechanics of the multinomial logistic regression we just reviewed, we can then apply it as the first solution to our digit classification project.

We first split the dataset into two subsets for training and testing respectively using the `caret` package.

caret stands for **classification and regression training**. The package is designed to facilitate the process for training and evaluating models. It contains tools and methods for data splitting, data pre-processing, feature selection and model tuning. Documentation and a full list of functions can be found in
`https://cran.r-project.org/web/packages/caret/caret.pdf`.

Install and import package `caret`:
```
> if (!require("caret"))
+ install.packages("caret")
> library (caret)
Loading required package: lattice
Loading required package: ggplot2
```

We first split the data into two partitions, 75% for training and 25% for testing, using the `createDataPartition` function:

```
> set.seed(42)
> train_perc = 0.75
> train_index <- createDataPartition(data$label, p=train_perc, list=FALSE)

> data_train <- data[train_index,]
> data_test <- data[-train_index,]
```

To ensure the experiments are reproducible, it is always a good practice to pick a seed from the random number generator.

Then, we implement the multinomial logistic regression model using the `nnet` package. The package contains functions for feed-forward single-layer neural networks as well as multinomial logistic regression models. More details can be found in https://cran.r-project.org/web/packages/nnet/nnet.pdf:

```
> library(nnet)
> # Multinomial logistic regression
> model_lr <- multinom(label ~ ., data=data_train, MaxNWts=10000,
decay=5e-3, maxit=100)
# weights: 7860 (7065 variable)
initial value 72538.338185
iter 10 value 17046.804658
iter 20 value 11166.225504
iter 30 value 9514.340319
iter 40 value 8819.724147
iter 50 value 8405.001712
iter 60 value 8164.997939
iter 70 value 7983.427139
iter 80 value 7897.005940
iter 90 value 7831.663204
iter 100 value 7730.047242
final value 7730.047242
stopped after 100 iterations
```

We fit a multinomial logistic regression model on the training subset, with parameters which include:

- `MaxNWts=10000`: It allows, at most, 10,000 weights. In our case, there are (784 dimensions + 1 bias) * 10 classes = 7850 elements in the weight matrix w
- `decay=5e-3`: The regularization strength, the weight decay is 0.005
- `maxit=100`: The maximum number of iterations is set to be 100

The error value is printed for every 10 iterations, and it is decreasing. The model converges as the maximum number of iterations is reached. Then we use the trained model to predict the classes of the testing samples:

```
> prediction_lr <- predict(model_lr, data_test, type = "class")
```

Take a look at the prediction results of the first five samples:

```
> prediction_lr[1:5]
[1] 1 0 7 5 8
Levels: 0 1 2 3 4 5 6 7 8 9
```

And their true values are:

```
> data_test$label[1:5]
[1] 1 0 7 5 8
Levels: 0 1 2 3 4 5 6 7 8 9
```

We can also obtain the confusion matrix by:

```
> cm_lr = table(data_test$label, prediction_lr)
> cm_lr
```

```
   prediction_lr
      0    1    2    3    4    5    6    7    8    9
0   965    0   11    4    1   12   23    6    7    4
1     0 1126    8    7    0    2    2    3   17    6
2     5   16  899   24   18    6   24   15   29    8
3     5    4   37  921    1   47    9   10   33   20
4     6   10    4    2  903    1   14    6   12   60
5    12    6    9   27    6  770   23    8   75   12
6     5    4   13    0   11    8  981    3    9    0
7     6    3   20    1    6    3    3  995    6   57
8     7   20    6   25    5   31    5    4  892   20
9     6    4    2   15   37    3    0   41   11  928
>
```

And the classification accuracy:

```
> accuracy_lr = mean(prediction_lr == data_test$label)
> accuracy_lr
[1] 0.8935886
```

89.4% for the first try. Not bad! We could definitely do better by tweaking the model parameters, such as decay and maxit. But our focus is for a more advanced model that learns the underneath patterns better. So we move on with the second solution, the feed-forward neural networks with a single hidden layer.

Going from logistic regression to single-layer neural networks

Basically, logistic regression is a feed-forward neural network without a hidden layer, where the output layer directly connects with the input layer. In other words, logistic regression is a single neuron that maps the input to the output layer. Theoretically, the neural networks with an additional hidden layer between the input and output layer should be able to learn more about the relationship underneath.

A single-layer neural network for two possible classes can be represented graphically as follows:

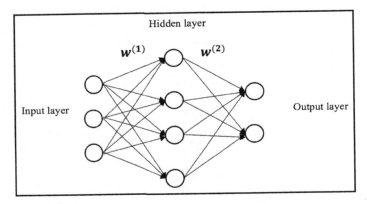

Suppose x is n-dimension, and there are H hidden units in the hidden layer, then the weight matrix $w^{(1)}$ connecting the input layer to the hidden layer is of size n by H with each column $w_h^{(1)}$ representing the coefficients associated with the h-th hidden unit. So, the output (also called **activation**) of the h-th hidden unit $a_h^{(2)}$ can be expressed mathematically as:

$$a_h^{(2)} = f(z^{(2)}) = f(w_h^{(1)}x)$$

For example, for the outputs of the first, second and the last hidden unit:

$$a_1^{(2)} = f(w_1^{(1)}x)$$

$$a_H^{(2)} = f(w_H^{(1)}x)$$

$$a_H^{(2)} = f(w_H^{(1)}x)$$

where $f(z)$ is an activation function. Typical choices for the activation function in simple networks include logistic function (more often called sigmoid function) and `tanh` function (which can be considered a re-scaled version of logistic function):

$$sigmoid(z) = \frac{1}{1 + e^{-z}}$$

$$tanh(z) = \frac{e^{-z} - e^{-z}}{e^z + e^{-z}} = \frac{2}{1 + e^{-2z}} - 1$$

Plots of these two functions are as follows:

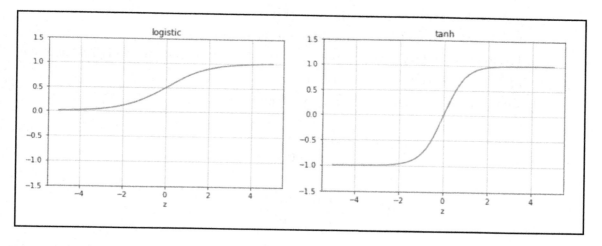

We will be using the logistic function in our single-layered networks for now.

For a case of K possible classes, the weight matrix $w^{(2)}$ connecting the hidden layer to the output layer is of size H by K. Each column $w_k^{(2)}$ represents the coefficients associated with class k. The input to the output layer is the output of the hidden layer $a^{(2)} = \{a_1^{(2)}, a_2^{(2)}, ...,a_1^{(2)}\}$, the probability of x being class k can be expressed mathematically as (for consistency, we denote it as $a_k^{(3)}$):

$$a_k^{(3)} = f(z^{(3)}) = softmax_k(W^{(2)}a^{(2)})$$

Similarly, given m training samples, to train the neural network, we learn all weights $w = \{w^{(1)}, w^{(2)}\}$ using gradient descent with the goal of minimizing the mean squared error cost $J(w)$.

Computation of the gradients Δw can be realized through the **backpropagation algorithm**. The idea of the backpropagation algorithm is the following, we first travel through the network and compute all outputs of the hidden layers and output layer; then moving backward from the last layer, we calculate how much each node contributed to the error in the final output and propagate it back to the previous layers. In our single-layer network, the detailed steps are:

1. Compute $a^{(2)}$ for the hidden layer and feed them to the output layer to compute the outputs $a^{(3)}$

2. For the output layer, compute the derivative of the cost function of one sample $j(W)$ with regards to each unit,
$$\delta_k^{(3)} = \frac{\delta}{\delta z_k^{(3)}} j(W) = -(y_k - a_k^{(3)}) . f'(z_k^{(3)})$$
, or
$\delta^{(3)} = -(y - a^{(3)}) . f'(z^{(3)})$, rewritten for the entire layer

3. For the hidden layer, we compute the error term $\delta^{(2)}$ based on a weighted average of $\delta^{(3)} : \delta^{(2)} = ((W^{(2)})^T \delta^{(3)}) . f'^{(2)})$

4. Compute the gradients applying the chain rule:

$$\triangle W^{(2)} = \frac{\partial J(W)}{\partial z_k^{(3)}} \frac{\partial z_k^{(3)}}{\partial W^{(2)}} = \delta^{(3)} (a^{(2)})^T$$

$$\triangle W^{(1)} = \frac{\partial J(W)}{\partial z_k^{(2)}} \frac{\partial z_k^{(2)}}{\partial W^{(1)}} = \delta^{(2)} (x)^T$$

We repeatedly update all weights by taking these steps until the cost function converges.

After a brief review of the single-layer network, we can then apply it as the second solution to our digit classification project.

Again, we use the `nnet` package to implement our single-layer network:

```
> model_nn <- nnet(label ~ ., data=data_train, size=50, maxit=300,
MaxNWts=100000, decay=1e-4)
# weights: 39760
initial value 108597.598656
iter 10 value 27708.286001
iter 20 value 16027.005297
iter 30 value 14058.141050
iter 40 value 12615.442747
iter 50 value 11793.700937
```

```
iter  60 value 11026.672273
iter  70 value 10654.855058
iter  80 value 10193.580947
iter  90 value 9854.836168
iter 100 value 9544.973159
iter 110 value 9307.192737
iter 120 value 9043.028253
iter 130 value 8845.069307
iter 140 value 8686.707561
iter 150 value 8525.104362
iter 160 value 8281.609223
iter 170 value 8140.051273
iter 180 value 7998.721024
iter 190 value 7854.388240
iter 200 value 7712.459027
iter 210 value 7636.945553
iter 220 value 7557.675909
iter 230 value 7449.854506
iter 240 value 7355.021651
iter 250 value 7259.186906
iter 260 value 7192.798089
iter 270 value 7055.027833
iter 280 value 6957.926522
iter 290 value 6866.641511
iter 300 value 6778.342997
final value 6778.342997
stopped after 300 iterations
```

We fit the model with parameters including:

- `size=50`: There are 50 hidden units in the hidden layer.
- `MaxNWts=100000`: It allows at most 100,000 weights. In our case, there are (784 input dimensions + 1 bias) * 50 hidden units = 39,250 elements in the weight matrix $w^{(1)}$ and (50 hidden units + 1 bias) * 10 output units = 510 elements in the weight matrix $w^{(1)}$. So there are 39,760 weights in total.
- `decay=1e-4`: The regularization strength, the weight decay is 0.0001.
- `maxit=300`: The maximum number of iterations is set to be 300.

We apply the trained network model on the testing set:

```
> prediction_nn <- predict(model_nn, data_test, type = "class")
> cm_nn = table(data_test$label, prediction_nn)
> cm_nn
prediction_nn
0 1 2 3 4 5 6 7 8 9
0 987 0 3 3 2 11 10 7 5 5
```

```
1  0  1134 9  6  0  2  0  5  11 4
2  14 9  918 31 11 11 7  15 22 6
3  3  1  17 966 0  41 3  14 24 18
4  4  3  8  2  929 4  11 11 5  41
5  12 2  6  17 5  851 15 9  26 5
6  10 1  14 0  9  14 970 0  15 1
7  4  4  23 6  5  2  0  1010 7  39
8  5  15 9  18 5  31 9  4  912 7
9  11 2  1  20 52 4  0  36 8  913
> accuracy_nn = mean(prediction_nn == data_test$label)
> accuracy_nn
[1] 0.9135944
```

Better than our first attempt! Can we do better with deep learning models, say intuitively more hidden layers? Sure.

Adding more hidden layers to the networks

We have just achieved 91.3% accuracy with a single-layer neural network model. Theoretically, we can obtain a better one with more than one hidden layer. As an example, we provide a solution of a deep neural network model with two hidden layers:

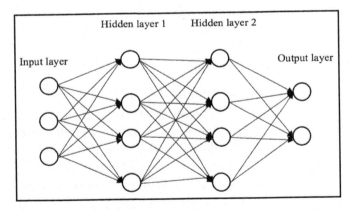

Weight optimization in feed-forward deep neural networks is also realized through the backpropagation algorithm, which is identical to single-layer networks. However, the more layers, the higher the computation complexity, and the slower the model convergence. One way to accelerate the weight optimization, is to use a more computational efficient activation function. The most popular one in recent years is the **rectified linear unit (ReLU)**:

$$relu(z) = z^+ = max(0, z)$$

A plot of the ReLU function is as follows:

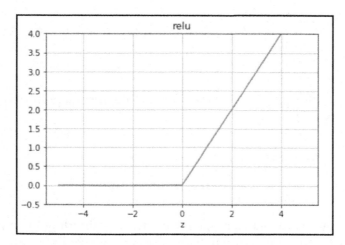

Thanks to the properties of its derivative, which is $relu'(z) = \begin{cases} 0, z < 0 \\ 1, z \geq 0 \end{cases}$, there are two main advantages of using the ReLU activation function over sigmoid:

- Faster learning because of constant value of *relu'(z)*, compared to that of the logistic function $sigmoid'(z) = sigmoid(z) * (1 - sigmoid(z))$.
- Less likely to have the vanishing gradient problem, exponential decrease of gradient, which can be found in networks with multiple stacked sigmoid layers. As we multiply the derivative of the activation function when calculating errors δ for each layer, and the maximal value of *sigmoid'(z)* is ¼, the gradients will decrease exponentially as we stack more and more sigmoid layers.

The nnet package we used in previous sections is (by now) only capable of modeling a single-layer network. In this chapter, we use the MXNet package to implement deep neural networks with multiple hidden layers. MXNet (https://mxnet.incubator.apache.org/) is a deep learning framework that supports programming languages include R, Scala, Python, Julia, C++, and Perl. It is developed by the DMLC (http://dmlc.ml/) team, a group of experts collaborating on open-source machine learning projects. It is portable and can scale to multiple CPUs, multiple GPUs and multiple machines, for example, in the cloud. Most importantly, it allows us to flexibly and efficiently construct state-of-the-art deep learning models, including deep neural networks, CNNs and RNNs.

Let's install MXNet first:

```
> cran <- getOption("repos")
> cran["dmlc"] <- "https://s3-us-west-2.amazonaws.com/apache-mxnet/R/CRAN/"
> options(repos = cran)
> if (!require("mxnet"))
install.packages("mxnet")
```

Now we can import MXNet and convert the data into the format preferred by the neural network models in MXNet:

```
> require(mxnet)
> data_train <- data.matrix(data_train)
> data_train.x <- data_train[,-1]
> data_train.x <- t(data_train.x/255)
> data_train.y <- data_train[,1]
```

Note we scale the input features to a range from 0 to 1, by dividing the maximal possible value 255. Otherwise, the deep neural networks may be skewed towards some features and such skewness will accumulate over layers.

Now that the training dataset is ready, we can start constructing the network by defining its architecture as follows:

```
> data <- mx.symbol.Variable("data")
> fc1 <- mx.symbol.FullyConnected(data, name="fc1", num_hidden=128)
> act1 <- mx.symbol.Activation(fc1, name="relu1", act_type="relu")
> fc2 <- mx.symbol.FullyConnected(act1, name="fc2", num_hidden=64)
> act2 <- mx.symbol.Activation(fc2, name="relu2", act_type="relu")
> fc3 <- mx.symbol.FullyConnected(act2, name="fc3", num_hidden=10)
> softmax <- mx.symbol.SoftmaxOutput(fc3, name="sm")
```

In the MXNet's Symbol API, we represent the network in the data type symbol. We begin with the input layer data, the input data, and follow up with the first hidden layer fc1 with 128 nodes, which fully connects with the input layer. We then attach the ReLU function to fc1 and output the activations act1 for this layer. Similarly, we chain another hidden layer fc2, with 64 nodes this time, and output ReLU-based activates act2. Finally, we end up with the output layer with a softmax function, generating 10 probabilities corresponding to 10 classes. The overall structure looks like this:

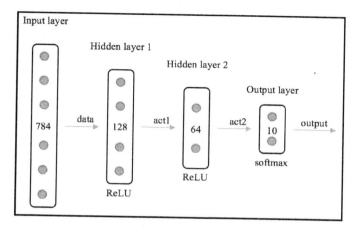

After building the bone, it is time to train the model. We can choose our computation device, CPU and/or GPU—here is a CPU example:

```
> devices <- mx.cpu()
```

Before training, don't forget to set the random seed to make the modeling process reproducible:

```
> mx.set.seed(42)
> model_dnn <- mx.model.FeedForward.create(softmax, X=data_train.x,
y=data_train.y, ctx=devices, num.round=30, array.batch.size=100,
learning.rate=0.01, momentum=0.9, eval.metric=mx.metric.accuracy,
initializer=mx.init.uniform(0.1),
epoch.end.callback=mx.callback.log.train.metric(100))
Start training with 1 devices
[1] Train-accuracy=0.724793650793651
[2] Train-accuracy=0.904715189873417
[3] Train-accuracy=0.925537974683544
[4] Train-accuracy=0.939936708860759
[5] Train-accuracy=0.950379746835443
[6] Train-accuracy=0.95873417721519
[7] Train-accuracy=0.96509493670886
[8] Train-accuracy=0.969905063291139
[9] Train-accuracy=0.974303797468355
[10] Train-accuracy=0.977784810126584
[11] Train-accuracy=0.980696202531648
[12] Train-accuracy=0.983164556962027
[13] Train-accuracy=0.985284810126584
[14] Train-accuracy=0.987405063291141
[15] Train-accuracy=0.988924050632913
[16] Train-accuracy=0.990727848101267
```

```
[17] Train-accuracy=0.992088607594938
[18] Train-accuracy=0.993227848101268
[19] Train-accuracy=0.994398734177217
[20] Train-accuracy=0.995284810126584
[21] Train-accuracy=0.995854430379748
[22] Train-accuracy=0.996835443037975
[23] Train-accuracy=0.997183544303798
[24] Train-accuracy=0.997848101265823
[25] Train-accuracy=0.998164556962026
[26] Train-accuracy=0.998575949367089
[27] Train-accuracy=0.998924050632912
[28] Train-accuracy=0.999177215189874
[29] Train-accuracy=0.999367088607595
[30] Train-accuracy=0.999525316455696
```

We just fit the model with hyperparameters including:

- `num.round = 30`: The maximum number of iterations is set to be 30.
- `array.batch.size = 100`: The batch size of the mini-batch gradient descent is 100. As a variation of a stochastic gradient descent, the mini-batch gradient descent algorithm calculates costs and gradients by small batches, instead of individual training samples. Hence, it is computationally more efficient and allows faster model convergence. As a result, the mini-batch gradient descent is more commonly used in training deep neural networks.
- `learning.rate = 0.01`: The learning rate is `0.01`.
- `momentum=0.9`: In general, the cost function of deep architectures has the form of one or more shallow ravines (local minima) leading to the global optimum. **Momentum** as seen in the physical law of motion is employed to avoid getting stuck in sub-optimum and make the convergence faster. With momentum, weights are updated as follows:

$$\nu = \gamma\nu - \eta\triangle W$$

$$W = W + \nu$$

where the left and right v is the previous and current velocity respectively, and $\gamma \in (0,1]$ is the momentum factor determining how much of the previous velocity is incorporated into the current one.

- `eval.metric=mx.metric.accuracy`: It uses classification accuracy as the evaluation metric

- `initializer=mx.init.uniform(0.1)`: Initial weights are randomly generated from the uniform distribution ranging from 0 to 1, so as to lower the chances of the weight exploding and vanishing in the deep network

After the model is trained, let's see how it performs on the testing set. First, remember to conduct the same pre-processing on the test dataset:

```
> data_test.x <- data_test[,-1]
> data_test.x <- t(data_test.x/255)
```

Then, predict the testing cases and evaluate the performance:

```
> prob_dnn <- predict(model_dnn, data_test.x)
> prediction_dnn <- max.col(t(prob_dnn)) - 1
> cm_dnn = table(data_test$label, prediction_dnn)
> cm_dnn
   prediction_dnn
        0    1    2    3    4    5    6    7    8    9
  0  1041    0    2    0    0    1    3    0    8    1
  1     0 1157    3    1    1    0    1    3    1    0
  2     2    1  993    3    3    1    2   13    5    2
  3     1    3   14 1033    1   13    0    5   14    6
  4     0    2    1    0  991    0    4    4    1   12
  5     4    2    3   12    3  892    4    3    6    8
  6    10    0    1    0    3    4  988    0    4    0
  7     0    5    9    1    2    0    0 1116    2    1
  8     4    8    3    5    0    8    3    2 1020   12
  9     1    1    0    4   13    3    0   16    2  957
> accuracy_dnn = mean(prediction_dnn == data_test$label)
> accuracy_dnn
[1] 0.9704706
```

By adding one more hidden layer, accuracy is improved from 91.4% to 97.0%! Since each hidden layer in a deep neural network provides representations of the data at a certain level, can we simply conclude that the more hidden layers (such as 100, 1,000, 10,000...), the more underneath patterns are discovered, the better the classification accuracy? It might be true if we have plentiful resources and time to enable computation and to make sure overfitting does not occur with such complex networks. Is there any way where we can extract richer and more informative representations than by simply chaining more hidden layers, and at the same time, not excessively grow our networks? The answer is CNNs.

Extracting richer representation with CNNs

Although regular hidden layers (we also call them fully connected layers) do the job of obtaining representations at certain levels, these representations might be able to help us differentiate between images of different classes. We need to extract richer and distinguishable representations that, for example, make a "9" a "9", a "4" a "4", or a cat a cat, a dog a dog. We resort to CNNs as variants of multi-layered neural networks which are biologically inspired by the human visual cortex. Basically, CNNs take inspiration from the following two neuroscience findings:

- The visual cortex has a complex system of neuronal cells that are sensitive to specific sub-regions of the visual field, called the **receptive field**. For instance, some cells respond only in the presence of vertical edges; some cells fire only when exposed to horizontal edges; and some react more strongly when shown edges of a certain orientation. The cells are organized together to produce the entire visual perception, while each individual cell is specialized in a specific component.
- Simple cells respond only when those edge-like patterns are presented within their receptive sub-regions. More complex cells are sensitive to larger sub-regions, and as a result, are less variant to the local position of those edge-like patterns in the entire visual field.

Similarly, CNNs classify images by first deriving low-level representations, local edges and curves, then by composing higher-level representations, overall shape and contour, through a series of low-level representations. CNNs are well suited to exploiting strong and unique features that differentiate between images.

In general, CNNs take in an image, pass it through a sequence of convolutional layers, non-linear layers, pooling layers and fully connected layers, and finally output the probabilities of each possible class. We now look at each type of layer individually, in detail.

The **convolutional layer** is the first layer in a CNN. It simulates the way neuronal cells respond to receptive fields by applying a convolutional operation to the input. To be specific, it computes the dot product between the weights of the convolutional layer and a small region they are connected to in the input layer. The small region is the receptive field, and the weights can be viewed as the values on a filter. As the filter slides from the beginning to the end of the input layer, the dot product between the weights and current receptive field is computed. A new layer called **feature map** is obtained after convolving over all sub-regions. Take a look at the following example:

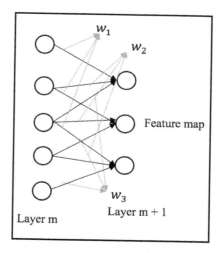

Layer *m* has five nodes and the filter has three units [w_1, w_2, w_3]. We compute the dot product between the filter and the first three nodes in layer *m* and obtain the first node in the feature map; then, we compute the dot product between the filter and the middle three nodes and generate the second node; finally, we obtain the third node resulting from the last three nodes in layer *m*.

Another example that helps us better understand how the convolutional layer works on images is as follows:

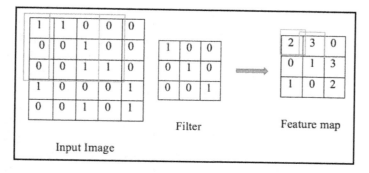

A 3*3 filter is sliding around a 5*5 image from the top left sub-region to the bottom right. For every sub-region, the dot product is computed with the filter. A 3*3 feature map is generated as a result.

Convolutional layers are actually used to extract features, such as edges and curves. The output pixel in the feature map will be of high value, if the corresponding receptive field contains an edge or curve specified by the filter. For instance, in the preceding example, the filter portrays a backslash-shape diagonal edge, the receptive field in the blue rectangle contains a similar curve and hence, the highest intensity 3 $(1*1 + 1*1 + 1*1 = 3)$ is produced; however, the receptive field in the bottom left corner does not contain such a shape, which results in a pixel of value 1. The convolutional layer acts as a curve detector, mimicking the way our visual cells work.

Remember in the preceding case, we only applied one filter and generated one feature map, which indicates how well the shape in the input image resembles the curve represented in the filter. To achieve a richer representation of the data, we can employ more filters, such as horizontal, vertical curve, 30-degree, or right-angle shape, so that the hidden layer composed of feature maps can detect more patterns. Additionally, stacking many convolutional layers can produce higher-level representations, such as overall shape and contour. To ensure the strong spatially local patterns are caught, each filter in a layer is only responsive to the corresponding receptive fields. Chaining more layers results in larger receptive fields which capture more global patterns.

Right after each convolutional layer, we often apply a **non-linear layer** (also called **activation layer**, as we mentioned), in order to introduce non-linearity, obviously. This is because only linear operations (multiplication and addition) are conducted in the convolutional layer. And a neural network with only linear hidden layers would behave just like a single-layer perceptron, regardless of how many layers. Again, ReLu is the most popular candidate for the non-linear layer in deep neural networks.

Normally, after obtaining features via one or more pairs of convolutional layers and non-linear layers, we can use the output for classification, for example applying a softmax layer in our multiclass case. Let's do some math, suppose we apply 20 5*5 filters in the first convolutional layer, then the output of this layer will be of size $20 * (28 - 5 + 1) * (28 - 5 + 1) = 20 * 24 * 24 = 11520$, which means the number of features as inputs for the next layer becomes 11,520 from 784; we then apply 50 5*5 filters in the second convolutional layer, the size of the output grows to $50 * 20 * (24 - 5 + 1) * (24 - 5 + 1) = 400,000$, which is high-dimensional compared to our initial size of 784. We can see that the dimension increases dramatically with each convolutional layer before the softmax layer for classification. This can easily lead to overfitting, not to mention the large number of weights to be trained in the corresponding non-linear layer.

To address the dimension growth issue, we often employ a **pooling layer** (also called **downsampling layer**) after a pair of convolutional and non-linear layers. As its name implies, it aggregates statistics of features by sub-regions to generate much lower dimensional features. Typical pooling methods include max pooling and mean pooling, which take the max values and mean values over all non-overlapping sub-regions, respectively. For example, we apply a 2*2 max pooling filter on a 4*4 feature map and output a 2*2 one:

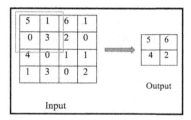

Besides reducing overfitting with lower dimensional output, the pooling layer aggregating statistics over regions has another advantage—translation invariant. It means the output does not change, if the input image undergoes a small amount of translation. For example, suppose we shift the input image to a couple of pixels left or right, up or down, as long as the highest pixels remain the same in sub-regions, the output of the max pooling layer is still the same. In another words, the prediction becomes less position-sensitive with pooling layers.

Putting these three types of convolutional-related layers together, along with fully connected layers, we can structure our CNN model as follows:

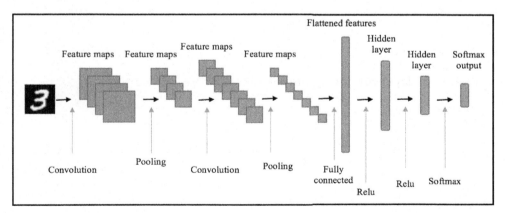

It starts with the first convolutional layer, ReLu non-linear layer and pooling layer. Here, we use 20 5*5 convolutional filters, and a 2*2 max pooling filter:

```
> # first convolution
> conv1 <- mx.symbol.Convolution(data=data, kernel=c(5,5),
num_filter=20)
> act1 <- mx.symbol.Activation(data=conv1, act_type="relu")
> pool1 <- mx.symbol.Pooling(data=act1, pool_type="max",
+ kernel=c(2,2), stride=c(2,2))
```

It follows with the second convolutional, ReLu non-linear and pooling layer, where 50 5*5 convolutional filters and a 2*2 max pooling filter are used:

```
> # second convolution
> conv2 <- mx.symbol.Convolution(data=pool1, kernel=c(5,5),
num_filter=50)
> act2 <- mx.symbol.Activation(data=conv2, act_type="relu")
> pool2 <- mx.symbol.Pooling(data=act2, pool_type="max",
+ kernel=c(2,2), stride=c(2,2))
```

Now that we extract rich representations of the input images by detecting edges, curves and shapes, we move on with the fully connected layers. But before doing so, we need to flatten the resulting feature maps from previous convolution layers:

```
> flatten <- mx.symbol.Flatten(data=pool2)
```

In the fully connected section, we apply two ReLu hidden layers with 500 and 10 units respectively:

```
> # first fully connected layer
> fc1 <- mx.symbol.FullyConnected(data=flatten, num_hidden=500)
> act3 <- mx.symbol.Activation(data=fc1, act_type="relu")
> # second fully connected layer
> fc2 <- mx.symbol.FullyConnected(data=act3, num_hidden=10)
```

Finally, the softmax layer producing outputs for 10 classes:

```
> # softmax output
> softmax <- mx.symbol.SoftmaxOutput(data=fc2, name="sm")
```

Now, the bone is constructed. Time to set a random seed and start training the model:

We need to first reshape the matrix, `data_train.x` into an array as required by the convolutional layer in MXNet:

```
> train.array <- data_train.x
> dim(train.array) <- c(28, 28, 1, ncol(data_train.x))
> mx.set.seed(42)
> model_cnn <- mx.model.FeedForward.create(softmax, X=train.array,
y=data_train.y, ctx=devices, num.round=30,
array.batch.size=100, learning.rate=0.05,
momentum=0.9, wd=0.00001,
eval.metric=mx.metric.accuracy,
epoch.end.callback=mx.callback.log.train.metric(100))
Start training with 1 devices
[1]  Train-accuracy=0.306984126984127
[2]  Train-accuracy=0.961898734177216
[3]  Train-accuracy=0.981139240506331
[4]  Train-accuracy=0.987151898734179
[5]  Train-accuracy=0.990348101265825
[6]  Train-accuracy=0.992689873417723
[7]  Train-accuracy=0.994493670886077
[8]  Train-accuracy=0.995822784810128
[9]  Train-accuracy=0.995601265822786
[10] Train-accuracy=0.997246835443039
[11] Train-accuracy=0.997341772151899
[12] Train-accuracy=0.998006329113925
[13] Train-accuracy=0.997626582278482
[14] Train-accuracy=0.998069620253165
[15] Train-accuracy=0.998765822784811
[16] Train-accuracy=0.998449367088608
[17] Train-accuracy=0.998765822784811
[18] Train-accuracy=0.998955696202532
[19] Train-accuracy=0.999746835443038
[20] Train-accuracy=0.999841772151899
[21] Train-accuracy=0.999905063291139
[22] Train-accuracy=1
[23] Train-accuracy=1
[24] Train-accuracy=1
[25] Train-accuracy=1
[26] Train-accuracy=1
[27] Train-accuracy=1
[28] Train-accuracy=1
[29] Train-accuracy=1
[30] Train-accuracy=1
```

Besides those hyperparameters we used in the previous deep neural network model, we fit the CNN model with L2 regularization weight decay `wd = 0.00001`, which adds penalties for large weights in order to avoid overfitting.

Again, training of the CNN model is no different to other networks. Optimal weights are obtained through a backpropagation algorithm.

After the model is trained, let's see how it performs on the testing set. First, remember to conduct the same pre-processing on the test dataset:

```
> test.array <- data_test.x
> dim(test.array) <- c(28, 28, 1, ncol(data_test.x))
```

Predict the testing cases and evaluate the performance:

```
> prob_cnn <- predict(model_cnn, test.array)
> prediction_cnn <- max.col(t(prob_cnn)) - 1
> cm_cnn = table(data_test$label, prediction_cnn)
> cm_cnn
prediction_cnn
  0    1    2    3    4   5    6    7    8   9
0 1051 0    1    0    0   1    1    0    2   0
1 0    1161 0    0    0   1    1    3    1   0
2 0    0    1014 4    0   0    0    7    0   0
3 0    0    2    1075 0   6    0    2    3   2
4 0    0    0    0    1000 0   4    2    2   7
5 1    0    0    4    0   923  3    0    3   3
6 3    0    0    0    0   0    1006 0    1   0
7 0    1    2    0    3   0    0    1129 1   0
8 3    3    1    1    2   5    1    0    1043 6
9 2    0    2    0    3   3    1    2    0   984
> accuracy_cnn = mean(prediction_cnn == data_test$label)
> accuracy_cnn
[1] 0.9893313
```

Our CNN model further boosts the accuracy to close to 99%!

We can also view the network structure by:

```
> graph.viz(model_cnn$symbol)
```

Let's do some more inspection to make sure we get things right. We start with the learning curving, for example the classification performance of the model on both the training set and testing set over the number of training iterations. In general, *it is a good practice to plot the learning curve where we can visualize whether overfitting or underfitting issues occur:*

```
> data_test.y <- data_test[,1]
> logger <- mx.metric.logger$new()
> model_cnn <- mx.model.FeedForward.create(softmax, X=train.array,
y=data_train.y,eval.data=list(data=test.array,
label=data_test.y), ctx=devices, num.round=30,
array.batch.size=100, learning.rate=0.05,
momentum=0.9, wd=0.00001,eval.metric=
mx.metric.accuracy, epoch.end.callback =
mx.callback.log.train.metric(1, logger))
Start training with 1 devices
[1] Train-accuracy=0.279936507936508
[1] Validation-accuracy=0.912857142857143
[2] Train-accuracy=0.959462025316456
[2] Validation-accuracy=0.973523809523809
[3] Train-accuracy=0.979841772151899
[3] Validation-accuracy=0.980666666666666
[4] Train-accuracy=0.986677215189875
[4] Validation-accuracy=0.983428571428571
[5] Train-accuracy=0.990822784810129
[5] Validation-accuracy=0.981809523809523
[6] Train-accuracy=0.992626582278482
[6] Validation-accuracy=0.983904761904761
[7] Train-accuracy=0.993322784810128
[7] Validation-accuracy=0.986
[8] Train-accuracy=0.995474683544305
[8] Validation-accuracy=0.987619047619047
[9] Train-accuracy=0.996487341772153
[9] Validation-accuracy=0.983904761904762
[10] Train-accuracy=0.995949367088608
[10] Validation-accuracy=0.984761904761904
[11] Train-accuracy=0.997310126582279
[11] Validation-accuracy=0.985142857142856
[12] Train-accuracy=0.997658227848102
[12] Validation-accuracy=0.986857142857142
[13] Train-accuracy=0.997848101265824
[13] Validation-accuracy=0.984095238095238
[14] Train-accuracy=0.998006329113924
[14] Validation-accuracy=0.985238095238094
[15] Train-accuracy=0.998607594936709
[15] Validation-accuracy=0.987619047619047
[16] Train-accuracy=0.99863924050633
[16] Validation-accuracy=0.987428571428571
```

```
[17]  Train-accuracy=0.998987341772152
[17]  Validation-accuracy=0.985142857142857
[18]  Train-accuracy=0.998765822784811
[18]  Validation-accuracy=0.986285714285713
[19]  Train-accuracy=0.999240506329114
[19]  Validation-accuracy=0.988761904761905
[20]  Train-accuracy=0.999335443037975
[20]  Validation-accuracy=0.98847619047619
[21]  Train-accuracy=0.999841772151899
[21]  Validation-accuracy=0.987809523809523
[22]  Train-accuracy=0.99993670886076
[22]  Validation-accuracy=0.990095238095237
[23]  Train-accuracy=1
[23]  Validation-accuracy=0.989999999999999
[24]  Train-accuracy=1
[24]  Validation-accuracy=0.989999999999999
[25]  Train-accuracy=1
[25]  Validation-accuracy=0.990190476190476
[26]  Train-accuracy=1
[26]  Validation-accuracy=0.990190476190476
[27]  Train-accuracy=1
[27]  Validation-accuracy=0.990095238095237
[28]  Train-accuracy=1
[28]  Validation-accuracy=0.990095238095237
[29]  Train-accuracy=1
[29]  Validation-accuracy=0.990095238095237
[30]  Train-accuracy=1
[30]  Validation-accuracy=0.990190476190475
```

We can get the performance on the training set after each round of training:

```
> logger$train
 [1] 0.2799365 0.9594620 0.9798418 0.9866772 0.9908228 0.9926266 0.9933228
 0.9954747 0.9964873 0.9959494 0.9973101
[12] 0.9976582 0.9978481 0.9980063 0.9986076 0.9986392 0.9989873 0.9987658
 0.9992405 0.9993354 0.9998418 0.9999367
[23] 1.0000000 1.0000000 1.0000000 1.0000000 1.0000000 1.0000000 1.0000000
 1.0000000
```

As well as the performance on the testing set after each round of training:

```
> logger$eval
 [1] 0.9128571 0.9735238 0.9806667 0.9834286 0.9818095 0.9839048 0.9860000
 0.9876190 0.9839048 0.9847619 0.9851429
[12] 0.9868571 0.9840952 0.9852381 0.9876190 0.9874286 0.9851429 0.9862857
 0.9887619 0.9884762 0.9878095 0.9900952
[23] 0.9900000 0.9900000 0.9901905 0.9901905 0.9900952 0.9900952 0.9900952
 0.9901905
```

The learning curve can be visualized by the following codes:

```
> plot(logger$train,type="l",col="red", ann=FALSE)
> lines(logger$eval,type="l", col="blue")
> title(main="Learning curve")
> title(xlab="Iterations")
> title(ylab="Accuary")
> legend(20, 0.5, c("training","testing"), cex=0.8,
col=c("red","blue"), pch=21:22, lty=1:2);
```

And we will get:

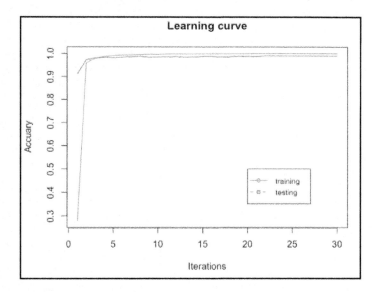

The learning curve indicates little chance of overfitting or underfitting.

Since the model works great, why don't we visualize the output of the convolutional layers of the trained model so that we can get a better understanding of CNNs. Let's use the first two samples in the testing set as an example. They are 1 and 0:

```
> par(mfrow=c(1,2))
> test_1 <- matrix(as.numeric(data_test[1,-1]), nrow = 28,
byrow = TRUE)
> image(rotate(test_1), col = grey.colors(255))
> test_2 <- matrix(as.numeric(data_test[2,-1]), nrow = 28,
byrow = TRUE)
> image(rotate(test_2), col = grey.colors(255))
```

For our reference, they are displayed as:

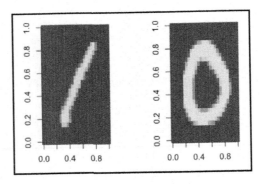

To visualize the activation of the convolutional layers, we first create an executor (can be loosely viewed as a copy of our trained CNN model) by grouping all of the layers with activations:

```
> layerss_for_viz <- mx.symbol.Group(mx.symbol.Group(c(conv1, act1, pool1,
conv2, act2, pool2, fc1, fc2)))
> executor <- mx.simple.bind(symbol=layerss_for_viz,
data=dim(test.array), ctx=mx.cpu())
```

Now, update the weights in the executor with those in the trained model:

```
> mx.exec.update.arg.arrays(executor, model_cnn$arg.params,
match.name=TRUE)
> mx.exec.update.aux.arrays(executor, model_cnn$aux.params,
match.name=TRUE)
```

And apply the executor on the testing set by making a feed-forward pass:

```
> mx.exec.update.arg.arrays(executor,
list(data=mx.nd.array(test.array)), match.name=TRUE)
> mx.exec.forward(executor, is.train=FALSE)
```

We can see the names of the layers recorded in the executor, as we will be extracting the activation of a layer by its name (note the names can be different, we should use the corresponding ones):

```
> names(executor$ref.outputs)
[1] "convolution10_output" "activation15_output"
"pooling10_output" "convolution11_output"
[5] "activation16_output" "pooling11_output"
"fullyconnected10_output" "fullyconnected11_output"
```

Now, we can visualize the activations for the first and second convolutional layer and ReLu layer, as well as the first pooling layer.

Let's start with the ReLu activations for the first 16 filters in the first convolutional layer, which are called `activation15_output` in our case (again, the name may vary). For the first sample, (a `"1"`), we run the following scripts:

```
> par(mfrow=c(4,4), mar=c(0.1,0.1,0.1,0.1))
> for (i in 1:16) {
+ outputData <- as.array
(executor$ref.outputs$activation15_output)[,,i,1]
+ image(outputData, xaxt='n', yaxt='n',
col=grey.colors(255)
+ )
+ }
```

Similarly, for the second sample, (a `"0"`), we run:

```
> par(mfrow=c(4,4), mar=c(0.1,0.1,0.1,0.1))
> for (i in 1:16) {
+ outputData <- as.array
(executor$ref.outputs$activation15_output)[,,i,2]
+ image(outputData, xaxt='n', yaxt='n',
col=grey.colors(255)
+ )
+ }
```

We plot the activations of the first convolutional layer for a 1 (left) and a 0 (right) input image, respectively:

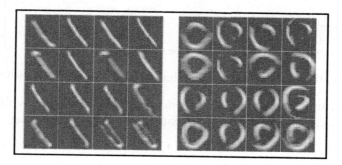

We can observe that each feature map effectively extracts the edges, curves and strikes of the digits.

We continue with the corresponding outputs of the first pooling layer called `pooling10_output`:

```
> par(mfrow=c(4,4), mar=c(0.1,0.1,0.1,0.1))
> for (i in 1:16) {
+ outputData <-as.array
(executor$ref.outputs$pooling10_output)[,,i,1]
+ image(outputData, xaxt='n', yaxt='n',
col=grey.colors(255)
+ )
+ }
> par(mfrow=c(4,4), mar=c(0.1,0.1,0.1,0.1))
> for (i in 1:16) {
+ outputData <- as.array
(executor$ref.outputs$pooling10_output)[,,i,2]
+ image(outputData, xaxt='n', yaxt='n',
col=grey.colors(255)
+ )
+ }
```

We plot the outputs of the first max pooling layer:

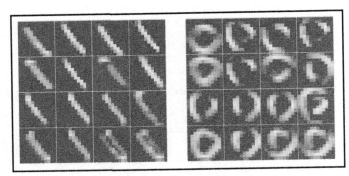

As we can easily tell, they are the downsampled versions of the convolution outputs.

Finally, we visualize one more layer, the second convolutional layer, which is labeled as `convolution11_output`. Take the first 16 feature maps as an example:

```
> par(mfrow=c(4,4), mar=c(0.1,0.1,0.1,0.1))
> for (i in 1:16) {
+ outputData <- as.array
(executor$ref.outputs$convolution11_output)[,,i,1]
+ image(outputData, xaxt='n', yaxt='n',
col=grey.colors(255)
+ )
```

```
+ }
> par(mfrow=c(4,4), mar=c(0.1,0.1,0.1,0.1))
> for (i in 1:16) {
+ outputData <- as.array
(executor$ref.outputs$convolution11_output)[,,i,2]
+ image(outputData, xaxt='n', yaxt='n',
col=grey.colors(255)
+ )
+ }
```

We plot the outputs of the second convolutional layer for two images, respectively:

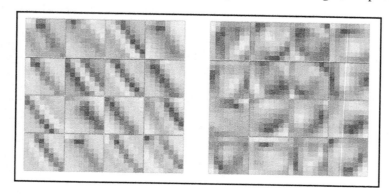

The second convolutional layer extracts higher-level features of the input images, such as shape and contour. All these 50 feature maps combined together, provide rich representations which are then fed into the fully connected layers. Therefore, classification performance is increased thanks to the convolution operations.

So far, we have examined the effectiveness of our CNN model by plotting the learning curve and visualizing the convolution extracted features. We can do one more inspection on the generalization of our model. For instance, we can take out a subset of data from the testing set to simulate a validation set, and use the remainder as the new testing set. We perform **early stopping** based on the validation set, which provides instruction on how many iterations is good enough and does not overfit the model. Finally, we employ the trained model with early stopping on the testing set and see how well the model is able to generalize to unseen data.

We first split the testing set into validation (40%) and final testing set (60%):

```
> validation_perc = 0.4
> validation_index <- createDataPartition(data_test.y, p=validation_perc,
list=FALSE)
>
```

```
> validation.array <- test.array[, , , validation_index]
> dim(validation.array) <- c(28, 28, 1,
length(validation.array[1,1,]))
> data_validation.y <- data_test.y[validation_index]
> final_test.array <- test.array[, , , -validation_index]
> dim(final_test.array) <- c(28, 28, 1,
length(final_test.array[1,1,]))
> data_final_test.y <- data_test.y[-validation_index]
```

To conduct early stopping, we write our custom callback function and will assign it to the parameter, `epoch.end.callback`. The callback function checks the classification performance on the validation set, and if it is greater than the threshold we set, the training stops:

```
> mx.callback.early.stop <- function(eval.metric) {
+ function(iteration, nbatch, env, verbose) {
+ if (!is.null(env$metric)) {
+ if (!is.null(eval.metric)) {
+ result <- env$metric$get(env$eval.metric)
+ if (result$value >= eval.metric) {
+ return(FALSE)
+ }
+ }
+ }
+ return(TRUE)
+ }
+ }
```

Now, we train the CNN model with early stopping based on the validation set where we set the stopping criteria as a validation accuracy greater than 0.985:

```
> model_cnn_earlystop <- mx.model.FeedForward.create(softmax,
X=train.array, y=data_train.y,
eval.data=list(data=validation.array, label=data_validation.y),
+ ctx=devices, num.round=30, array.batch.size=100,
+ learning.rate=0.05, momentum=0.9, wd=0.00001,
eval.metric=mx.metric.accuracy,
+ epoch.end.callback = mx.callback.early.stop(0.985))
Start training with 1 devices
[1] Train-accuracy=0.284571428571429
[1] Validation-accuracy=0.921395348837209
[2] Train-accuracy=0.959145569620254
[2] Validation-accuracy=0.972325581395349
[3] Train-accuracy=0.980221518987343
[3] Validation-accuracy=0.97906976744186
[4] Train-accuracy=0.986613924050634
[4] Validation-accuracy=0.982790697674419
```

```
[5] Train-accuracy=0.990537974683546
[5] Validation-accuracy=0.981627906976744
[6] Train-accuracy=0.992848101265824
[6] Validation-accuracy=0.985348837209302
```

Training stops after the sixth iteration as the criteria is met. Finally, the performance on the new testing set is examined:

```
> prob_cnn <- predict(model_cnn_earlystop, final_test.array)
> prediction_cnn <- max.col(t(prob_cnn)) - 1
> cm_cnn = table(data_final_test.y, prediction_cnn)
> cm_cnn
                 prediction_cnn
data_final_test.y   0   1   2   3   4   5   6   7   8   9
                0 626   0   0   0   0   0   0   0   1   0
                1   0 701   1   0   0   2   1   3   4   0
                2   1   0 598   4   0   0   0   6   0   0
                3   0   0   0 658   0   5   0   0   2   1
                4   0   0   0   0 585   1   3   3   1   4
                5   1   0   1   3   0 558   5   0   0   2
                6   4   0   0   0   0   0 595   0   0   0
                7   0   1   3   0   1   0   0 675   0   0
                8   4   0   1   1   1   7   3   0 621   2
                9   1   0   0   0   2   1   0   4   0 589
> accuracy_cnn = mean(prediction_cnn == data_final_test.y)
> accuracy_cnn
[1] 0.9855487
```

Our CNN model is able to generalize decently.

Summary

We have just finished our first mile in the R and deep learning journey! Through this chapter, we got more familiar with the important concepts of deep learning. We started with what deep learning is all about, why it is important and the recent success of applications, as well. After we were well equipped, we solved the handwritten digit using shallow neural networks, deep neural networks and CNNs in sequence, and proved that CNNs are the best suited to exploiting strong and unique features that differentiate images of different classes.

Inspired by the human visual cortex, CNNs classify images by first deriving rich representations such as edges, curves and shapes, which was demonstrated in the visualization of the outputs of convolutional layers. In addition, we verified the performance and generalization of the CNN model using early stopping as a technique to avoid overfitting. Overall, we not only covered the mechanics of CNNs, including the concepts of convolution and pooling, but also implemented a CNN model with `MXNet`, as one of the most popular deep learning packages in R.

2
Traffic Sign Recognition for Intelligent Vehicles

Convolutional neural networks (CNNs) are so useful in computer vision that we are going to use one for another application, traffic sign detection for intelligent vehicles. We will also cover several important concepts of deep learning in this chapter and will get readers exposed to other popular frameworks and libraries for deep learning.

We continue our R deep learning journey with one of the core problems in self-driving cars, object recognition, and to be specific, traffic sign classification. To avoid accidents and ensure safety, robust traffic sign classification is critical to realizing driving autonomy. We will start with what self-driving cars are and what aspects deep learning is applied to. We will also discuss how deep learning stands out and becomes the state-of-the-art solution for object recognition in intelligent vehicles. With the background knowledge in mind, we'll get started with our project when we first conduct an exploratory analysis of the data and performance data preprocessing, including Y'UV color encoding conversion. We'll make our first attempt at using CNNs with MXNet and achieve more than 99% accuracy. Then we'll move on to another powerful deep learning framework called TensorFlow and an API built on top of it called Keras.

We'll also introduce the dropout technique as a regularization approach similar to Lasso (L1) / Ridge (L2) regularization. Besides overfitting, we'll demonstrate how to deal with a lack of training data, utilizing data augmentation techniques. We'll wrap up the chapter by summarizing approaches to prevent overfitting in CNN models. Once again, we will prove that deep learning models remove manual or explicit feature extraction steps that are taken in traditional approaches, and they instead automatically discover useful patterns underneath input data during the training process.

We will get into the details of the topics mentioned here:

- What self-driving cars are
- How deep learning is applied in self-driving cars
- How deep learning becomes a state-of-the-art solution for object recognition in intelligent vehicles
- Exploratory analysis on the German Traffic Sign Recognition Benchmark dataset's data
- Traffic sign recognition using convolutional neural networks with the MXNet package
- Keras and TensorFlow
- Traffic sign recognition using convolutional neural networks with the `keras` package
- Reducing overfitting with dropout
- Data augmentation and common augmentation methods
- Using data augmentation for a small training set
- Summarizing approaches to prevent overfitting in CNN models

How is deep learning applied in self-driving cars?

A self-driving car (also called an autonomous/automated vehicle or driverless car) is a robotic vehicle that is capable of traveling between destinations and navigating without human intervention. To enable autonomy, self-driving cars detect and interpret environments using a variety of techniques such as radar, GPS and computer vision; and they then plan appropriate navigational paths to the desired destination.

In more detail, the following is how self-driving cars work in general:

- The software plans the routes based on the destination, traffic, and road information and starts the car
- A **Light Detection and Ranging** (**LiDAR**) sensor captures the surroundings in real time and creates a dynamic 3D map
- Sensors monitor lateral movement to calculate the car's position on the 3D map

- Radar systems exploit information on distances from other traffic participants, pedestrians, or obstacles
- Computer vision algorithms recognize traffic signs, traffic lights, and other landmarks from a camera and provide advance notices
- The algorithm-driven software analyzes all sensory data, combines inputs from other sources, and controls actions such as steering and braking, simulating the way humans perceive the surroundings and make decisions

How does deep learning become a state-of-the-art solution?

As we can see, robust object recognition is critical to realizing driving autonomy. To avoid accidents and ensure safety, it is necessary to be attentive to the surrounding environment, traffic signs, and lights. Generally speaking, object recognition in self-driving cars can be summarized into four tasks:

- Object detection, such as obstacles, pedestrians, traffic signs, and lights.
- Object identification and classification. An example is of labeling traffic lights (red, yellow, green, and off) if detected in the images captured by the frontal camera. Then we have categorizing of traffic participants into bicycle, motorcycle, car, truck and bus, and of course classifying traffic signs (our main talking point in this chapter).
- Object localization, which maps ground-level images to aerial imagery.
- Movement prediction, for example, understanding the speed of an object or estimating the behavior and intention of a pedestrian based on his/her pose.

Since the past two decades, a variety of machine learning algorithms have been applied to solve object recognition problems in intelligent vehicles.

For example, in *Detecting Pedestrians Using Patterns of Motion and Appearance* (Viola et al., published in the International Journal of Computer Vision, 63(2)), the **AdaBoost** (short for **Adaptive Boosting**, which corrects classification errors sequentially) classifier was employed to detect walking pedestrians.

In *Histograms of Oriented Gradients for Human Detection* (Dalal and Triggs, published in the IEEE Conference on Computer Vision and Pattern Recognition (CVPR) in 2005), efficient features were extracted using the **histogram of orientation** (**HOG**) technique, and fed into a **support vector machine** (**SVM**) classifier for human detection. Since then, more sophisticated variants such as gradient field HOG (GF-HOG) and other more complex feature extraction methods were developed. To name some, we have zoning + projection, projection + HOG, and so on.

Conventional object recognition approaches (explicit feature extraction + machine learning classification) rely heavily on hand-crafted features, such as gradient orientation histogram with HOG, local keypoints with **Sped-Up Robust Features** (**SURF**), or **Scale Invariant Feature Transform** (**SIFT**). Although they perform well in certain tasks, designing these feature descriptors is difficult and requires lots of manual tweaks and experiments.

Recall that in the previous chapter on classifying handwritten digits, we resorted to a CNN. It first derives low-level representations, local edges and curves, and then composes higher level representations such as overall shape and contour through a series of low-level representations. We also concluded that CNNs are well suited to exploit strong and unique features.

In fact, it has been proven in many solutions that CNNs are able to efficiently automate feature extraction while allowing a significant boost in performance. For example, in *Pedestrian Detection with Unsupervised Multi-Stage Feature Learning* (Sermanet et al., published in the IEEE Conference on **Computer Vision and Pattern Recognition** (**CVPR**) in 2013), CNNs were first introduced into the pedestrian detection problem. In *Rich feature hierarchies for accurate object detection and semantic segmentation* (Girshick et al., published in the IEEE Conference on CVPR in 2014), a variant region-based CNN model was proposed to improve performance. Nowadays, a number of state-of-the-art object recognition approaches involve deep learning techniques, CNNs specifically. A good testimony would be their prevalence in top positions in the leaderboard of the KITTI Vision Benchmark for autonomous cars (`http://www.cvlibs.net/datasets/kitti/eval_object.php?obj_benchmark=2d`).

I hope all of these cases have excited you about CNNs and their power of providing better object recognition solutions to intelligent vehicles.

So what are we waiting for? Let's proceed with our project, traffic signs recognition, as it is one of the most important topics in autonomous cars!

Traffic sign recognition using CNN

As always, we begin by exploring the **German Traffic Sign Recognition Benchmark** (**GTSRB**) dataset at `http://benchmark.ini.rub.de/?section=gtsrb&subsection=dataset`.

Getting started with exploring GTSRB

The GTSRB dataset, compiled and generously published by the real-time computer vision research group in Institut für Neuroinformatik, was originally used for a competition of classifying single images of traffic signs. It consists of a training set of 39,209 labeled images and a testing test of 12,630 unlabeled images. The training dataset contains 43 classes—43 types of traffic signs. We will go through all classes and exhibit several samples for each class.

The dataset can be downloaded via `http://benchmark.ini.rub.de/Dataset/GTSRB_Final_Training_Images.zip` (located in the **Downloads | Training dataset** section on the page). Unzip the downloaded file and there will be a folder called `Images` containing 43 folders (`00000, 00001`... up to `00042`); they represent 43 classes of images. These images are in the following form:

- The image files are in **PPM** (short for **portable pixmap**) format.
- The number of images from each class ranges from 210 to 2250. So it is an unbalanced multi-class classification problem.
- Each image contains one traffic sign.
- The sizes of the images are not uniform, ranging from 15*15 to 250*250 pixels, and images are not necessarily square.
- Images contain a border of up to 10% around the actual sign. Thus the sign is not necessarily centered with the image.

Let's start by plotting a sample, `00000_00002.ppm`, in the `00000` folder.

We use the `pixmap` package (`https://cran.r-project.org/web/packages/pixmap`) to read the PPM file:

```
> library('pixmap')
> image <-
read.pnm('GTSRB/Final_Training/Images/00000/00000_00002.ppm',cellres=1)
```

Now we obtain a `pixmapRGB` object with attributes `red`, `green`, and `blue` (which are the pixels for each of the three channels), as well as `size`, which is the width and height of the image. And we can access the red, green, and blue channel as follows:

```
> red_matrix <- matrix(image@red, nrow = image@size[1], ncol =
image@size[2])
> green_matrix <- matrix(image@green, nrow = image@size[1], ncol =
image@size[2])
> blue_matrix <- matrix(image@blue, nrow = image@size[1], ncol =
image@size[2])
```

We visualize the original image and its three channels individually:

```
> plot(image, main=sprintf("Original"))
> rotate <- function(x) t(apply(x, 2, rev))
> par(mfrow=c(1, 3))
> image(rotate(red_matrix), col = grey.colors(255), main=sprintf("Red"))
> image(rotate(green_matrix), col = grey.colors(255),
main=sprintf("Green"))
> image(rotate(blue_matrix), col = grey.colors(255), main=sprintf("Blue"))
```

Note that here we reuse the rotate function we defined in the last chapter to better view the images. This is an original image:

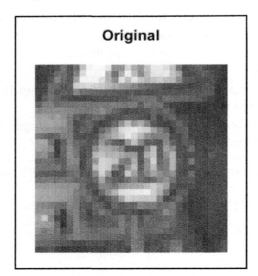

The following images show the output for the red, blue, and green channel, respectively:

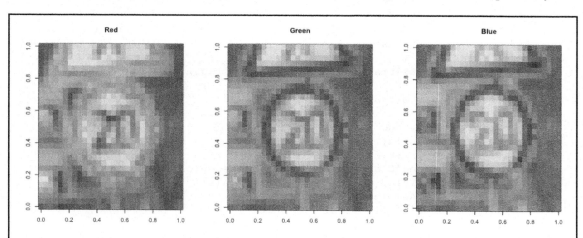

It is a 20 km/h speed limit sign.

We can now go through 43 classes of signs and display three samples for each type by defining the following function:

```
> plot_samples <- function(training_path, class, num_sample){
+     classes <- c("Speed limit (20km/h)", "Speed limit (30km/h)",
                 "Speed limit (50km/h)", "Speed limit (60km/h)",
+                "Speed limit (70km/h)", "Speed limit (80km/h)",
                 "End of speed limit (80km/h)",
+                "Speed limit (100km/h)", "Speed limit (120km/h)",
                 "No passing",
+                "No passing for vehicles over 3.5 metric tons",
                 "Right-of-way at the next intersection",
+                "Priority road", "Yield", "Stop", "No vehicles",
                 "Vehicles over 3.5 metric tons prohibited",
+                "No entry", "General caution", "Dangerous curve to
                 the left", "Dangerous curve to the right",
+                "Double curve", " Bumpy road", "Slippery road",
                 "Road narrows on the right", "Road work",
+                "Traffic signals", "Pedestrians", "Children
                 crossing", "Bicycles crossing",
                 "Beware of ice/snow",
+                "Wild animals crossing",
                 "End of all speed and passing limits",
                 "Turn right ahead",
+                "Turn left ahead", "Ahead only",
```

```
                         "Go straight or right", "Go straight or left",
                         "Keep right", "Keep left", "Roundabout mandatory",
                         "End of no passing",
+                        "End of no passing by vehicles over 3.5 metric
                          tons")
+       if (class<10) {
+         path <- paste(training_path, "0000", class, "/", sep="")
+       } else {
+         path <- paste(training_path, "000", class, "/", sep="")
+       }
+       par(mfrow=c(1, num_sample))
+       # Randomly display num_sample samples
+       all_files <- list.files(path = path)
+       title <- paste('Class', class, ':', classes[class+1])
+       print(paste(title, "             (", length(all_files),
+                 " samples)", sep=""))
+       files <- sample(all_files, num_sample)
+       for (file in files) {
+         image <- read.pnm(paste(path, file, sep=""), cellres=1)
+         plot(image)
+       }
+       mtext(title, side = 3, line = -23, outer = TRUE)
+ }
```

Call the function with `class=0`:

```
> training_path <- "GTSRB/Final_Training/Images/"
> plot_samples(training_path, 0, 3)
[1] "Class 0 : Speed limit (20km/h)          (211 samples)"
```

Three samples are displayed:

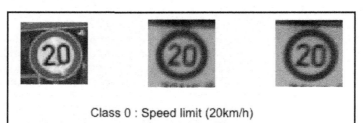

Class 0 : Speed limit (20km/h)

Repeat this function call with a different class (or use a loop) to go through the remaining 42 types:

```
> plot_samples(training_path, 1, 3)
[1] "Class 1 : Speed limit (30km/h)          (2221 samples)"
```

Three samples from class 1 are displayed as follows:

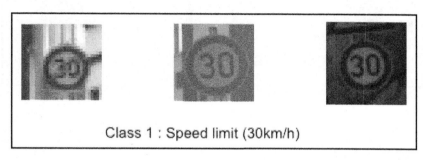

Class 1 : Speed limit (30km/h)

```
> plot_samples(training_path, 2, 3)
[1] "Class 2 : Speed limit (50km/h)          (2251 samples)"
```

Three images from class 2 are shown here:

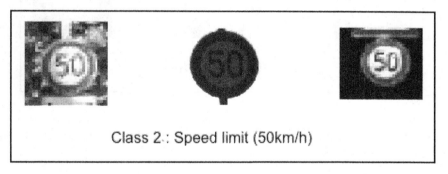

Class 2 : Speed limit (50km/h)

```
> plot_samples(training_path, 3, 3)
[1] "Class 3 : Speed limit (60km/h)          (1411 samples)"
```

Here is the result for class 3:

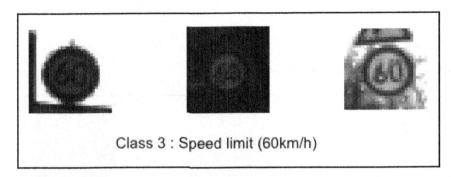

Class 3 : Speed limit (60km/h)

```
> plot_samples(training_path, 4, 3)
[1] "Class 4 : Speed limit (70km/h)        (1981 samples)"
```

We plot three images from class 4:

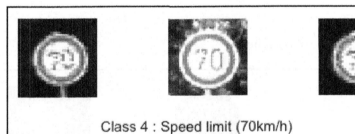

Class 4 : Speed limit (70km/h)

Here we skip the remainder, but it is clear that the images were captured under various conditions, including weather, illumination, occlusion, rotations, and so on. Instead, we list all types of sample sizes for easy reference:

ID	Type	Number of samples
0	Speed limit (20km/h)	211
1	Speed limit (30km/h)	2221
2	Speed limit (50km/h)	2251
3	Speed limit (60km/h)	1411
4	Speed limit (70km/h)	1981

5	Speed limit (80km/h)	1861
6	End of speed limit (80km/h)	421
7	Speed limit (100km/h)	1441
8	Speed limit (120km/h)	1411
9	No passing	1471
10	No passing for vehicles over 3.5 metric tons	2011
11	Right-of-way at the next intersection	1321
12	Priority road	2101
13	Yield	2161
14	Stop	781
15	No vehicles	631
16	Vehicles over 3.5 metric tons prohibited	421
17	No entry	1111
18	General caution	1201
19	Dangerous curve to the left	211
20	Dangerous curve to the right	361
21	Double curve	331
22	Bumpy road	391
23	Slippery road	511
24	Road narrows on the right	271
25	Road work	1501
26	Traffic signals	601
27	Pedestrians	241
28	Children crossing	541
29	Bicycles crossing	271
30	Beware of ice/snow	451
31	Wild animals crossing	781

32	End of all speed and passing limits	241
33	Turn right ahead	690
34	Turn left ahead	421
35	Ahead only	1201
36	Go straight or right	391
37	Go straight or left	211
38	Keep right	2071
39	Keep left	301
40	Roundabout mandatory	361
41	End of no passing	241
42	End of no passing by vehicles over 3.5 metric tons	241

Obviously, the signs, our **regions of interest (ROI)**, are not centered within the images, whose sizes unfortunately vary. As a result, we need to separate the ROI from the image and standardize its size (resizing it to 32*32 as most researchers have done) before we can analyze and classify the data. We resort to the annotations provided along with the images. Each class folder contains an annotation file, for example, `GT-00000.csv` located at `00000`. Each annotation file contains the following useful fields:

- `Filename`: The filename of the image
- `ROI.X1`: The x coordinate of the top-left corner of the ROI bounding box
- `ROI.Y1`: The y coordinate of the top-left corner of the ROI bounding box
- `ROI.X2`: The x coordinate of the bottom-right corner of the ROI bounding box
- `ROI.Y2`: The y coordinate of the bottom-right corner of the ROI bounding box

Here is an example of the ROI in a sample:

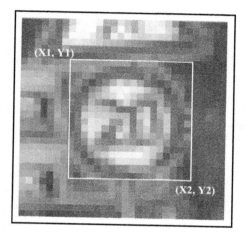

Now we define the preprocessing function for a raw image, which includes separating the ROI and resizing it to 32*32:

```
> source("http://bioconductor.org/biocLite.R")
> biocLite("EBImage")
> library("EBImage")
> roi_resize <- function(input_matrix, roi){
+     roi_matrix <- input_matrix[roi[1, 'Roi.Y1']:roi[1, 'Roi.Y2'],
                  roi[1, 'Roi.X1']:roi[1, 'Roi.X2']]
+     return(resize(roi_matrix, 32, 32))
+ }
```

Note that the resize function is from the EBImage package:

```
https://bioconductor.org/packages/release/bioc/html/EBImage.html
```

We try it out on our first sample (red channel only):

```
> # read annotation csv file
> annotation <-
read.csv(file="GTSRB/Final_Training/Images/00000/GT-00000.csv",
header=TRUE, sep=";")
> roi = annotation[3, ]
> red_matrix_cropped <- roi_resize(red_matrix, roi)
> par(mfrow=c(1, 2))
> image(rotate(red_matrix), col = grey.colors(255) ,
main=sprintf("Original"))
> image(rotate(red_matrix_cropped), col = grey.colors(255) ,
main=sprintf("Preprocessed"))
```

We get the preprocessed red channel on the right:

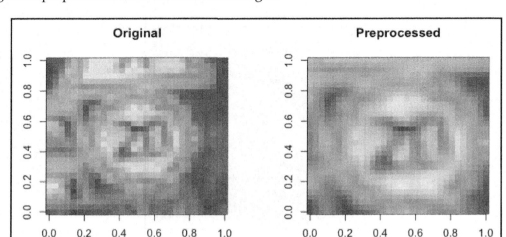

Similarly, we can process the other two channels. Based on these three channels, how can we construct the feature space? Discarding any channel might result in loss of information. Simply stacking them up could lead to redundancy. So, combining three channels into one would be a better solution. In the color world, Y'UV is an encoding system that encrypts brightness information separately from color information. It is typically used as part of a color image pipeline and computer graphics hardware. Y'UV represents human perception of color in terms of three components: Y' as the luminance (brightness), and U and V as the chrominance (color). Y'UV can be converted from RGB using:

- $Y' = 0.299R + 0.587G + 0.114B$
- $U = 0.492(B - Y')$
- $V = 0.877(R - Y')$

For our feature space, we can only take the brightness channel Y'.

Now that we have the last piece of the whole preprocessing ready, let's put them together, load, and process (ROI + resize + conversion to Y') the entire labeled dataset:

```
> load_labeled_data <- function(training_path, classes){
+    # Initialize the pixel features X and target y
+    X <- matrix(, nrow = 0, ncol = 32*32)
+    y <- vector()
+    # Load images from each of the 43 classes
+    for(i in classes) {
+       print(paste('Loading images from class', i))
```

```
+      if (i<10) {
+        annotation_path <- paste(training_path, "0000", i, "/GT-0000",
                              i, ".csv", sep="")
+      path <- paste(training_path, "0000", i, "/", sep="")
+      } else {
+        annotation_path <- paste(training_path, "000", i, "/GT-000",
                              i, ".csv", sep="")
+      path <- paste(training_path, "000", i, "/", sep="")
+      }
+      annotation <- read.csv(file=annotation_path, header=TRUE,
                          sep=";")
+
+      for (row in 1:nrow(annotation)) {
+        # Read each image
+        image_path <- paste(path, annotation[row, "Filename"], sep="")
+        image <- read.pnm(image_path, cellres=1)
+        # Parse RGB color space
+        red_matrix <- matrix(image@red, nrow = image@size[1],
                          ncol = image@size[2])
+        green_matrix <- matrix(image@green, nrow = image@size[1],
                          ncol = image@size[2])
+        blue_matrix <- matrix(image@blue, nrow = image@size[1],
                          ncol = image@size[2])
+        # Crop ROI and resize
+        red_matrix_cropped <- roi_resize(red_matrix,
                                    annotation[row, ])
+        green_matrix_cropped <- roi_resize(green_matrix,
                                    annotation[row, ])
+        blue_matrix_cropped <- roi_resize(blue_matrix,
                                    annotation[row, ])
+        # Convert to brightness, e.g. Y' channel
+        x <- 0.299 * red_matrix_cropped + 0.587 *
                green_matrix_cropped + 0.114 * blue_matrix_cropped
+        X <- rbind(X, matrix(x, 1, 32*32))
+        y <- c(y, i)
+      }
+
+      }
+
+    return(list("x" = X, "y" = y))
+ }
```

After defining the data loading function as shown previously, we apply it to the entire raw dataset:

```
> classes <- 0:42
> data <- load_labeled_data(training_path, classes)
```

Be patient as it might take a couple of hours to read and process 39,209 images. Just in case anything unexpected happens, a good practice is to save the data object so that we can restore it anytime later:

```
> # Save the data object to a file
> saveRDS(data, file = "43 classes.rds")
> # Restore the data object
> data <- readRDS(file = "43 classes.rds")
```

Just do a quick check on the ready-to-use data:

```
> data.x <- data$x
> data.y <- data$y
> dim(data.x)
[1] 39209  1024
```

Correct dimension!

```
> summary(as.factor(data.y))
     0     1     2     3     4     5     6     7     8     9    10    11    12    13    14
    15    16    17    18    19    20    21    22
   210  2220  2250  1410  1980  1860   420  1440  1410  1470  2010  1320  2100  2160   780
   630   420  1110  1200   210   360   330   390
    23    24    25    26    27    28    29    30    31    32    33    34    35    36    37
    38    39    40    41    42
   510   270  1500   600   240   540   270   450   780   240   689   420  1200   390   210
  2070   300   360   240   240
```

Correct class sizes, and again they are rather unbalanced!

 Never skip checking the class balance for classification.

After ensuring that the data is loaded and processed properly, we do more exploratory analysis on the distribution of features, that is, the pixels. As an example, we take the 16 pixels from the central 4*4 block (222nd to 225th, 254th to 257th, 286th to 289th, and 318th to 321st) in each image from class 1 (Speed limit=30km/h), 14 (Stop), 20 (Dangerous curve to the right), and 27 (Pedestrians). We display their histograms:

```
> central_block <- c(222:225, 254:257, 286:289, 318:321)
> par(mfrow=c(2, 2))
> for(i in c(1, 14, 20, 27)) {
+    hist(c(as.matrix(data.x[data.y==i, central_block])),
+         main=sprintf("Histogram for class %d", i),
```

```
+          xlab="Pixel brightness")
+ }
```

The resulting pixel brightness histograms are displayed as follows:

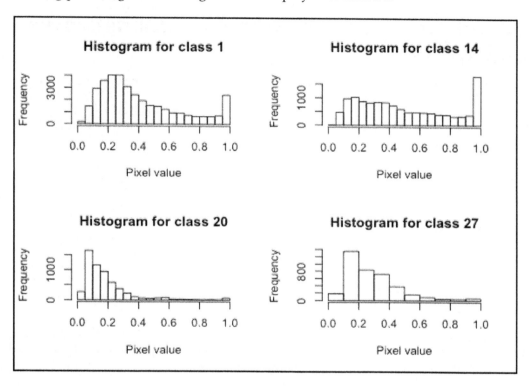

The brightness of the central pixels is distributed differently among these four classes. For instance, the majority of the central pixels from class 20 are dark, as the sign (Dangerous curve to the right) has a thick black stroke through the center; while in class 14, the stop sign has a white stroke (the left part of the **O**) near the central area. Pixels taken from other positions can also be distinctly distributed among different classes.

The exploratory analysis we just conducted helps us to move forward with building classification models based on pixels.

First solution – convolutional neural networks using MXNet

We start off with a solution similar to the one we developed at the end of the previous chapter, with CNNs using MXNet.

Again, we first split the dataset into two subsets for training (75%) and testing (25%) using the `caret` package:

```
> if (!require("caret"))
+      install.packages("caret")
> library (caret)
> set.seed(42)
> train_perc = 0.75
> train_index <- createDataPartition(data.y, p=train_perc, list=FALSE)
> train_index <- train_index[sample(nrow(train_index)),]
> data_train.x <- data.x[train_index,]
> data_train.y <- data.y[train_index]
> data_test.x <- data.x[-train_index,]
> data_test.y <- data.y[-train_index]
```

Don't forget to specify a particular random seed for reproducible work. We normally do data normalization before applying CNNs. In our case, the raw pixels loaded are already in the range of 0 to 1; after Y' brightness conversion, the resulting pixels are still in the range of 0 to 1.

In general, normalizing our data is necessary before putting it into a CNN or in fact any neural network or gradient-descent-based model. As for image inputs, we usually scale the pixels in the range of 0 to 1.

After preparing the training and testing set, we structure our CNN model as follows:

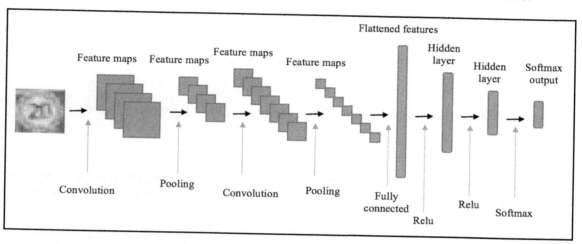

The network starts with the first set of convolutional layers, the ReLu nonlinear layer and the pooling layer. Here we use 32 5*5 convolutional filters and a 2*2 max pooling filter:

```
> require(mxnet)
> data <- mx.symbol.Variable("data")
> # first convolution
> conv1 <- mx.symbol.Convolution(data=data, kernel=c(5,5),
                              num_filter=32)
> act1 <- mx.symbol.Activation(data=conv1, act_type="relu")
> pool1 <- mx.symbol.Pooling(data=act1, pool_type="max",
+                         kernel=c(2,2), stride=c(2,2))
```

It follows with the second set of convolutional, ReLu nonlinear and pooling layer, where 64 5*5 convolutional filters and 2*2 max pooling filter are used:

```
> # second convolution
> conv2 <- mx.symbol.Convolution(data=pool1, kernel=c(5,5),
                              num_filter=64)
> act2 <- mx.symbol.Activation(data=conv2, act_type="relu")
> pool2 <- mx.symbol.Pooling(data=act2, pool_type="max",
+                         kernel=c(2,2), stride=c(2,2))
```

Now that we've extracted rich representations of the input images by detecting edges, curves, and shapes, we move on to the fully connected layers. But before doing so, we need to flatten the resulting feature maps from the previous convolution layers:

```
> flatten <- mx.symbol.Flatten(data=pool2)
```

In the fully connected section, we apply a ReLu hidden layer with 1,000 units and a softmax layer with 43 units:

```
> # first fully connected layer
> fc1 <- mx.symbol.FullyConnected(data=flatten, num_hidden=1000)
> act3 <- mx.symbol.Activation(data=fc1, act_type="relu")
> # second fully connected layer
> fc2 <- mx.symbol.FullyConnected(data=act3, num_hidden=43)
```

Finally, the softmax layer, producing outputs for each of the 43 classes:

```
> # softmax output
> softmax <- mx.symbol.SoftmaxOutput(data=fc2, name="sm")
```

All pieces of the network are now assembled. Before we start training the model, we specify the random seed and training devices and reshape the matrix `data_train.x` into an array as required by the convolutional layer in MXNet:

```
> devices <- mx.cpu()
> train.array <- t(data_train.x)
> dim(train.array) <- c(32, 32, 1, nrow(data_train.x))
> mx.set.seed(42)
```

Time for model training:

```
> model_cnn <- mx.model.FeedForward.create(softmax, X=train.array,
y=data_train.y, ctx=devices, num.round=30,
array.batch.size=100, learning.rate=0.05, momentum=0.9,
wd=0.00001, eval.metric=mx.metric.accuracy,
                epoch.end.callback=mx.callback.log.train.metric(100))
```

Start training with one device:

```
[1]  Train-accuracy=0.184965986394558
[2]  Train-accuracy=0.824610169491525
[3]  Train-accuracy=0.949389830508475
[4]  Train-accuracy=0.968305084745763
[5]  Train-accuracy=0.983050847457628
[6]  Train-accuracy=0.988372881355934
[7]  Train-accuracy=0.990745762711866
[8]  Train-accuracy=0.993152542372882
[9]  Train-accuracy=0.992576271186442
[10] Train-accuracy=0.994372881355933
[11] Train-accuracy=0.99542372881356
[12] Train-accuracy=0.995118644067798
[13] Train-accuracy=0.99671186440678
[14] Train-accuracy=0.999830508474576
[15] Train-accuracy=0.999932203389831
```

```
[16]  Train-accuracy=1
[17]  Train-accuracy=1
[18]  Train-accuracy=1
[19]  Train-accuracy=1
[20]  Train-accuracy=1
[21]  Train-accuracy=1
[22]  Train-accuracy=1
[23]  Train-accuracy=1
[24]  Train-accuracy=1
[25]  Train-accuracy=1
[26]  Train-accuracy=1
[27]  Train-accuracy=1
[28]  Train-accuracy=1
[29]  Train-accuracy=1
[30]  Train-accuracy=1
```

We just fit our model with hyperparameters:

- `num.round =30`: The maximum number of iterations
- `array.batch.size = 100`: The batch size of mini-batch gradient descent
- `learning.rate = 0.05`: The learning rate
- `momentum=0.9`: The momentum factor that determines how much of the previous velocity is incorporated into the current one
- `eval.metric=mx.metric.accuracy`: This uses classification accuracy as the evaluation metric
- `initializer=mx.init.uniform(0.1)`: Initial weights are randomly generated from the uniform distribution between -0.1 and 0.1 so as to lower the chances of weights exploding and vanishing in the deep network
- `wd = 0.00001`: The weight decay for L2 regularization, which adds penalties for large weights in order to avoid overfitting

We can view the structure of the model by:

```
> graph.viz(model_cnn$symbol)
```

The trained model is then applied to the testing set:

```
> test.array <- t(data_test.x)
> dim(test.array) <- c(32, 32, 1, nrow(data_test.x))
> prob_cnn <- predict(model_cnn, test.array)
> prediction_cnn <- max.col(t(prob_cnn)) - 1
```

We compute the confusion matrix and classification accuracy as follows:

```
> cm_cnn = table(data_test.y, prediction_cnn)
> cm_cnn
```

The first half of the resulting confusion matrix:

prediction_cnn data_test.y	0	1	2	3	4	5	6	7	8	9	10	11	12	13	14	15	16	17	18	19	20	21	22	23	24
0	39	0	0	0	0	0	0	0	0	0	0	0	0	0	0	0	0	0	0	0	0	0	0	0	0
1	0	551	1	0	0	0	0	0	0	0	0	0	0	1	0	0	0	0	0	0	0	0	0	0	0
2	0	0	589	0	1	0	0	1	0	0	0	0	0	0	0	0	0	0	0	0	0	0	0	0	0
3	0	0	0	336	0	1	0	0	0	0	0	0	0	0	0	0	0	0	0	0	0	0	0	1	0
4	0	0	0	0	505	0	0	0	0	0	0	0	0	0	0	0	0	0	0	0	0	0	0	0	0
5	0	0	0	0	0	453	0	0	0	0	0	0	0	0	0	1	0	0	0	0	0	0	0	0	0
6	0	0	0	0	0	0	95	1	0	0	0	0	0	0	0	0	0	0	0	0	0	0	0	0	0
7	0	0	1	1	0	2	0	362	0	0	0	0	0	0	0	0	0	0	0	0	0	0	0	0	0
8	0	0	0	0	0	0	0	0	356	0	1	0	0	0	1	0	0	0	0	0	0	0	0	0	0
9	0	0	0	0	0	0	0	0	0	357	0	0	0	0	1	0	0	0	0	0	0	0	0	0	0
10	0	0	0	0	0	1	0	0	0	1	505	0	0	0	0	0	0	0	0	0	0	0	0	0	0
11	0	0	0	0	0	0	0	0	0	0	0	311	0	0	0	0	0	0	0	0	0	0	0	0	0
12	0	0	0	0	0	0	0	0	0	0	0	0	539	0	0	2	0	0	0	0	0	0	0	0	0
13	0	1	1	0	0	0	0	0	0	1	1	1	1	513	0	0	0	0	1	0	0	0	0	0	0
14	0	0	0	1	0	0	0	0	0	0	0	0	0	0	194	0	0	0	0	0	0	0	0	0	0
15	0	1	0	0	0	0	0	0	0	0	0	0	2	0	0	170	0	0	0	0	0	0	0	0	0
16	0	0	0	0	0	0	0	0	0	0	0	0	0	0	0	0	113	0	0	0	0	0	0	0	0
17	0	0	0	0	0	0	0	0	0	0	0	0	0	0	0	0	0	285	0	0	0	0	0	0	0
18	0	0	0	0	0	0	0	0	0	0	0	1	0	0	0	0	0	0	308	0	0	0	0	0	0
19	0	0	0	0	0	0	0	0	0	0	0	0	0	0	0	0	0	0	0	57	0	0	0	0	0
20	0	0	0	0	0	0	0	0	0	0	0	0	0	0	0	0	0	0	1	3	77	0	0	0	0
21	0	0	0	0	0	0	0	0	0	0	0	0	0	0	0	0	0	0	0	0	0	82	0	0	0
22	0	0	0	0	0	0	0	0	0	0	0	0	0	0	0	0	0	0	0	0	0	0	79	0	0
23	0	0	0	0	0	0	0	0	0	0	0	0	0	0	0	0	0	0	1	0	0	0	1	135	0
24	0	0	0	0	0	0	0	0	0	0	0	0	0	0	0	0	0	0	1	0	0	0	0	0	66
25	0	0	0	0	0	0	0	0	0	0	0	0	0	0	0	0	0	0	0	0	0	0	0	0	0
26	0	0	0	0	0	0	0	0	0	0	1	0	0	0	0	0	0	0	1	0	1	0	0	0	0
27	0	0	0	0	0	0	0	0	0	0	0	0	0	0	0	0	0	0	0	0	0	0	0	0	1
28	0	0	0	0	0	0	0	0	0	0	0	0	0	0	0	0	0	0	0	1	0	0	0	0	0
29	0	0	0	0	0	0	0	0	0	0	0	0	0	0	0	0	0	0	0	0	0	0	0	0	1
30	0	0	0	0	0	1	0	0	0	0	0	0	0	0	0	0	0	0	0	0	0	0	0	0	0
31	0	0	0	0	0	0	0	0	0	0	0	0	0	0	0	0	0	0	0	0	0	0	0	0	0
32	0	0	0	0	0	0	0	0	0	0	0	0	0	0	0	0	0	0	0	0	0	0	0	0	0
33	0	0	0	0	0	0	0	0	0	0	0	0	0	0	0	0	0	0	0	0	0	0	0	0	0
34	0	0	1	0	0	0	0	0	0	0	0	0	0	0	0	0	0	0	0	0	0	0	0	0	0
35	0	0	0	0	0	0	0	0	0	0	0	0	0	0	0	0	0	0	0	0	0	0	0	0	0
36	0	0	0	0	0	0	0	0	0	0	0	0	0	0	0	0	0	0	0	0	1	0	0	0	0
37	0	0	0	0	0	0	0	0	0	0	1	0	0	0	0	0	0	0	0	0	0	0	0	0	0
38	0	0	0	0	0	0	0	0	0	0	0	0	0	0	0	0	0	0	0	0	0	0	0	0	0
39	0	0	0	0	0	0	0	0	0	0	0	0	0	0	0	0	0	0	0	0	0	0	0	0	0
40	0	0	0	0	0	0	0	0	0	0	0	0	0	0	0	0	0	0	0	0	0	0	0	0	0
41	0	0	0	0	0	0	0	0	0	0	0	0	0	0	0	0	0	0	0	0	0	0	0	0	0
42	0	0	0	1	0	0	0	0	0	0	0	0	0	0	0	0	0	0	0	0	0	0	0	0	0

The second half:

data_test.y	prediction_cnn																	
	25	26	27	28	29	30	31	32	33	34	35	36	37	38	39	40	41	42
0	0	0	0	0	0	0	0	0	0	0	0	0	0	0	0	0	0	0
1	0	0	0	0	0	0	0	0	0	0	0	0	0	0	0	0	0	0
2	0	0	0	0	0	0	0	0	0	0	0	0	0	0	0	0	0	0
3	0	0	0	0	0	0	0	0	0	0	0	0	0	0	0	0	0	0
4	0	0	0	0	0	0	0	0	0	0	0	0	0	0	0	0	0	0
5	0	0	0	0	0	0	0	0	0	0	0	0	1	1	0	0	0	0
6	0	0	0	0	0	0	0	0	0	0	0	0	0	0	0	0	0	0
7	0	0	0	0	0	0	0	0	0	0	0	0	0	0	0	1	0	0
8	0	0	0	0	0	0	0	0	0	0	0	0	0	0	0	0	0	0
9	0	0	0	0	0	0	0	0	0	0	0	0	0	0	0	1	0	0
10	0	1	0	0	0	0	0	0	0	0	0	0	0	0	0	0	0	0
11	0	0	0	0	0	1	0	0	0	0	0	0	0	0	0	0	0	0
12	0	0	0	0	0	0	0	0	0	0	1	0	0	0	0	0	0	0
13	0	0	0	0	0	0	0	0	0	0	0	0	0	0	0	0	0	0
14	0	0	0	0	0	0	0	0	0	0	0	0	0	0	0	0	0	0
15	0	0	0	0	0	0	0	0	0	0	0	0	0	0	0	0	0	0
16	0	0	0	0	0	0	0	0	0	0	0	0	0	0	0	0	0	0
17	0	0	0	0	0	0	0	0	0	0	0	0	0	0	0	0	0	0
18	1	0	0	0	0	0	0	0	0	0	0	0	0	0	0	0	0	0
19	0	0	0	0	0	0	0	0	0	0	0	0	0	0	0	0	0	0
20	0	0	0	2	0	0	0	0	0	0	0	0	0	0	0	0	0	0
21	1	0	0	0	0	0	0	0	0	0	0	0	0	0	0	0	0	0
22	0	0	0	0	0	0	0	0	0	0	0	0	0	0	0	0	0	0
23	0	0	0	0	1	0	0	0	0	0	0	0	0	0	0	0	0	0
24	0	0	0	0	1	0	0	0	0	0	0	0	0	0	1	0	0	0
25	363	0	0	0	0	0	0	0	0	0	0	0	0	0	0	0	0	0
26	0	150	0	0	0	0	0	0	0	0	0	0	0	0	0	0	0	0
27	0	0	57	0	0	0	0	0	0	0	0	0	0	0	0	0	0	0
28	0	0	0	131	0	0	0	0	0	0	0	0	0	0	0	0	0	0
29	0	0	0	0	65	0	0	0	0	0	0	0	0	0	0	0	0	0
30	0	0	0	0	0	122	0	0	0	0	0	0	0	0	0	0	0	0
31	0	0	0	0	0	0	198	0	0	0	0	0	0	0	0	0	0	0
32	0	0	0	0	0	0	0	47	0	0	0	0	0	0	0	0	0	0
33	0	0	0	0	0	0	0	0	181	1	0	0	0	0	0	0	0	0
34	0	0	0	0	0	0	0	0	0	110	0	0	0	0	0	0	0	0
35	1	0	0	0	0	0	0	0	0	0	288	1	0	0	0	0	0	0
36	1	0	0	1	0	0	0	0	0	0	0	95	0	0	0	0	0	0
37	0	0	0	0	0	0	0	0	0	0	0	0	40	0	0	0	0	0
38	0	0	0	0	0	0	0	0	0	0	0	0	0	499	0	0	0	0
39	0	0	0	0	0	0	0	0	0	0	0	0	0	0	74	0	0	0
40	0	0	0	0	0	0	0	0	0	0	0	0	0	0	0	94	0	0
41	0	0	0	0	0	0	0	1	0	0	0	0	0	0	0	0	71	0
42	0	0	0	0	0	0	0	0	0	0	0	0	0	0	0	0	0	70

Misclassification occurs only in several rare cases regardless of large variations in appearances of images due to illumination changes, partial occlusions, rotations, weather conditions, and so on:

```
> accuracy_cnn = mean(prediction_cnn == data_test.y)
> accuracy_cnn
[1] 0.9930612
```

We just built a robust CNN model that correctly classifies more than 99.30% of the testing signs. The CNN model efficiently learns the representations by deriving low-level and high-level features. It makes those hand-crafted features obsolete, as it captures important and distinguishable features by itself from the sign images.

Now that we have achieved great success using our favorite (so far) deep learning tool MXNet, why don't we explore other tools that are also powerful? In fact, another deep learning API called Keras has been gaining popularity recently; its backend, TensorFlow, is probably the best known deep learning framework.

Trying something new – CNNs using Keras with TensorFlow

Keras (https://keras.io/) is a high-level deep learning API written in Python that can run on top of any of these three deep learning frameworks: TensorFlow (from Google), CNTK (from Microsoft), and Theano (from the Montreal Institute for Learning Algorithms, Université de Montréal, Canada). To solve a machine learning problem efficiently, being able to quickly prototype ideas is the key. And this is why Keras was developed initially, to facilitate fast experimentation in the following key aspects:

- User-friendly API built on top of multiple powerful backends, including TensorFlow, CNTK, and Theano.
- Built-in CNN, RNN, and autoencoder models as well as support classes and methods (metrics, optimizers, regularizers, visualization, and so on), which enable easy and fast prototyping.
- Excellent modularity and extensibility. These allow for customized network architectures: Multiple input, multiple output, layer sharing, model sharing, memory-based network, and so on.
- Allowing the same code to run seamlessly on CPU and GPU.

For R users, the R interface to Keras (`https://keras.rstudio.com/`) was developed in 2017, and its adoption by the community has gradually grown. Let's first install the `keras` R package from GitHub as follows:

```
> if (!require("keras"))
+     devtools::install_github("rstudio/keras")
> library(keras)
```

This is not finished yet. We need to install the underlying backend(s) that Keras connects to. By default, it uses TensorFlow as the backend engine. We can use the following function to install the TensorFlow backend:

```
> install_keras()
Using existing virtualenv at  ~/.virtualenvs/r-tensorflow
Upgrading pip ...
......
Installation complete.
```

While we are waiting for the installation, let's learn a bit more about TensorFlow.

TensorFlow (`https://www.tensorflow.org/`) is an open source machine learning framework created by Google. It is well known for being used to design, build, and train deep learning models, but it can also be used for general numerical computation. In TensorFlow, computation is described using data flow graphs, where each node in a graph represents an instance of a mathematical operation and each edge represents a multidimensional data array (the so-called tensor, which can hold a matrix, vector, or scalar) on which the operations are performed. Such flexible architecture allows us to efficiently perform data-crunching machine learning operations, such as derivatives on huge matrices. Here is an example of a data flow graph:

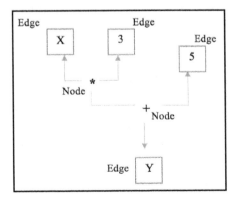

Now we see where its name TensorFlow is derived from: Tensors flowing in networks.

By now, the installation of the core Keras library as well as the TensorFlow backend is done. We continue our Keras-based solution for traffic signs classification.

First, prepare the input data for Keras modeling by reshaping the training and testing feature matrix:

```
> x_train <- data_train.x
> dim(x_train) <- c(nrow(data_train.x), 32, 32, 1)
> x_test <- data_test.x
> dim(x_test) <- c(nrow(data_test.x), 32, 32, 1)
```

Again, the input pixels are already of values ranging from 0 to 1, so we do not need to perform any rescaling.

We also convert training and testing target vectors (integers from 0 to 42) into a binary class matrix (one-hot encoded) as required by the Keras classification models:

```
> y_train <- to_categorical(data_train.y, num_classes = 43)
> y_test <- to_categorical(data_test.y, num_classes = 43)
```

Before we start modeling, there is a trick for obtaining reproducible results in Keras in R. It is specifying a random seed before development of a model using the following function:

```
> use_session_with_seed(42)
```

It takes all measures known to ensure reproducible results from Keras sessions.

Time to define the model after data preparation!

We begin by initializing the Keras sequential model as follows:

```
> model <- keras_model_sequential()
```

Then we add the first set of convolutional layers, the ReLu nonlinear layer and the pooling layer, with the same parameters used in the previous MXNet solution (same parameters are used for rest of the network):

```
> model %>%
```

Start with a hidden 2D convolutional layer being fed 32*32 pixel images:

```
+    layer_conv_2d(
+      filter = 32, kernel_size = c(5,5),
+      input_shape = c(32, 32, 1)
+    ) %>%
+    layer_activation("relu") %>%
+    layer_max_pooling_2d(pool_size = c(2,2)) %>%
```

Note that we use the pipe (%>%) operator to add layers to the Keras sequential model.

It follows with the second set of convolutional, ReLu nonlinear, and pooling layer:

```
+    # Second hidden convolutional layer layer
+    layer_conv_2d(filter = 64, kernel_size = c(5,5)) %>%
+    layer_activation("relu") %>%
+    layer_max_pooling_2d(pool_size = c(2,2)) %>%
```

Flatten the resulting feature maps from the previous convolution layers:

```
+    layer_flatten() %>%
```

And feed into a dense layer:

```
+    layer_dense(1000) %>%
+    layer_activation("relu") %>%
```

Finally, connect to a softmax layer containing 43 output units:

```
+    layer_dense(43) %>%
+    layer_activation("softmax")
```

We can use the `summary()` function to view the details of the model:

```
> summary(model)
```

```
--------------------------------------------------------------------------
Layer (type)                     Output Shape              Param #
==========================================================================
conv2d_1 (Conv2D)                (None, 28, 28, 32)        832
--------------------------------------------------------------------------
activation_1 (Activation)        (None, 28, 28, 32)        0
--------------------------------------------------------------------------
max_pooling2d_1 (MaxPooling2D)   (None, 14, 14, 32)        0
--------------------------------------------------------------------------
conv2d_2 (Conv2D)                (None, 10, 10, 64)        51264
--------------------------------------------------------------------------
activation_2 (Activation)        (None, 10, 10, 64)        0
--------------------------------------------------------------------------
max_pooling2d_2 (MaxPooling2D)   (None, 5, 5, 64)          0
--------------------------------------------------------------------------
flatten_1 (Flatten)              (None, 1600)              0
--------------------------------------------------------------------------
dense_1 (Dense)                  (None, 1000)              1601000
--------------------------------------------------------------------------
activation_3 (Activation)        (None, 1000)              0
--------------------------------------------------------------------------
dense_2 (Dense)                  (None, 43)                43043
--------------------------------------------------------------------------
activation_4 (Activation)        (None, 43)                0
==========================================================================
Total params: 1,696,139
Trainable params: 1,696,139
Non-trainable params: 0
--------------------------------------------------------------------------
```

Depending on when the model is constructed, the names of the layers may have different suffixes (_1, _2 for example).

All the pieces of the CNN model are now assembled. Before compiling the model, we need to explicitly specify its optimizer. In MXNet, the optimizer is a parameter in the `mx.model.FeedForward.create` method with **stochastic gradient descent (SGD)** as the default value. In Keras, we use the same optimizer with the same learning rate and momentum:

```
> opt <- optimizer_sgd(lr = 0.005, momentum = 0.9)
```

Along with the optimizer we just defined, cross entropy as the loss function, and classification accuracy as the metric, we compile the CNN model:

```
> model %>% compile(
+    loss = "categorical_crossentropy",
+    optimizer = opt,
+    metrics = "accuracy"
+ )
```

We can now safely kick off our model training. Again, the same hyperparameters are used, including batch size and number of iterations. Note that the testing dataset is used for model validation, where the classification performance of the current CNN model is computed for each training iteration. Last but not least, shuffle is not necessary in our case as the training data is already shuffled after raw data splits:

```
> model %>% fit(
+    x_train, y_train,
+    batch_size = 100,
+    epochs = 30,
+    validation_data = list(x_test, y_test),
+    shuffle = FALSE
+ )
Train on 29409 samples, validate on 9800 samples
Epoch 1/30
29409/29409 [==============================] - 109s 4ms/step - loss: 2.8031
- acc: 0.2823 - val_loss: 1.1719 - val_acc: 0.6733
Epoch 2/30
29409/29409 [==============================] - 109s 4ms/step - loss: 0.6438
- acc: 0.8372 - val_loss: 0.4079 - val_acc: 0.8891
Epoch 3/30
29409/29409 [==============================] - 110s 4ms/step - loss: 0.3154
- acc: 0.9217 - val_loss: 0.2623 - val_acc: 0.9336
Epoch 4/30
29409/29409 [==============================] - 109s 4ms/step - loss: 0.1969
- acc: 0.9533 - val_loss: 0.2096 - val_acc: 0.9483
Epoch 5/30
29409/29409 [==============================] - 24703s 840ms/step - loss:
0.1410 - acc: 0.9682 - val_loss: 0.1715 - val_acc: 0.9604
Epoch 6/30
29409/29409 [==============================] - 1076s 37ms/step - loss:
0.1055 - acc: 0.9761 - val_loss: 0.1363 - val_acc: 0.9690
Epoch 7/30
29409/29409 [==============================] - 34344s 1s/step - loss:
0.0860 - acc: 0.9806 - val_loss: 0.1147 - val_acc: 0.9742
Epoch 8/30
29409/29409 [==============================] - 104s 4ms/step - loss: 0.0698
- acc: 0.9841 - val_loss: 0.1065 - val_acc: 0.9756
```

```
Epoch 9/30
29409/29409 [==============================] - 108s 4ms/step - loss: 0.0535
- acc: 0.9874 - val_loss: 0.1015 - val_acc: 0.9780
Epoch 10/30
29409/29409 [==============================] - 109s 4ms/step - loss: 0.0414
- acc: 0.9913 - val_loss: 0.0927 - val_acc: 0.9801
Epoch 11/30
29409/29409 [==============================] - 108s 4ms/step - loss: 0.0415
- acc: 0.9917 - val_loss: 0.0912 - val_acc: 0.9807
Epoch 12/30
29409/29409 [==============================] - 106s 4ms/step - loss: 0.0341
- acc: 0.9933 - val_loss: 0.1054 - val_acc: 0.9769
Epoch 13/30
29409/29409 [==============================] - 108s 4ms/step - loss: 0.0266
- acc: 0.9946 - val_loss: 0.0811 - val_acc: 0.9842
Epoch 14/30
29409/29409 [==============================] - 106s 4ms/step - loss: 0.0207
- acc: 0.9965 - val_loss: 0.0790 - val_acc: 0.9845
Epoch 15/30
29409/29409 [==============================] - 106s 4ms/step - loss: 0.0221
- acc: 0.9955 - val_loss: 0.0780 - val_acc: 0.9841
Epoch 16/30
29409/29409 [==============================] - 109s 4ms/step - loss: 0.0169
- acc: 0.9974 - val_loss: 0.0753 - val_acc: 0.9854
Epoch 17/30
29409/29409 [==============================] - 109s 4ms/step - loss: 0.0137
- acc: 0.9982 - val_loss: 0.0777 - val_acc: 0.9863
Epoch 18/30
29409/29409 [==============================] - 109s 4ms/step - loss: 0.0114
- acc: 0.9986 - val_loss: 0.0757 - val_acc: 0.9863
Epoch 19/30
29409/29409 [==============================] - 109s 4ms/step - loss: 0.0101
- acc: 0.9990 - val_loss: 0.0775 - val_acc: 0.9867
Epoch 20/30
29409/29409 [==============================] - 108s 4ms/step - loss: 0.0086
- acc: 0.9993 - val_loss: 0.0786 - val_acc: 0.9862
Epoch 21/30
29409/29409 [==============================] - 110s 4ms/step - loss: 0.0077
- acc: 0.9994 - val_loss: 0.0776 - val_acc: 0.9859
Epoch 22/30
29409/29409 [==============================] - 110s 4ms/step - loss: 0.0071
- acc: 0.9995 - val_loss: 0.0774 - val_acc: 0.9862
Epoch 23/30
29409/29409 [==============================] - 109s 4ms/step - loss: 0.0066
- acc: 0.9996 - val_loss: 0.0779 - val_acc: 0.9862
Epoch 24/30
29409/29409 [==============================] - 110s 4ms/step - loss: 0.0062
- acc: 0.9997 - val_loss: 0.0783 - val_acc: 0.9860
```

```
Epoch 25/30
29409/29409 [==============================] - 114s 4ms/step - loss: 0.0059
- acc: 0.9997 - val_loss: 0.0786 - val_acc: 0.9859
Epoch 26/30
29409/29409 [==============================] - 115s 4ms/step - loss: 0.0056
- acc: 0.9998 - val_loss: 0.0791 - val_acc: 0.9861
Epoch 27/30
29409/29409 [==============================] - 117s 4ms/step - loss: 0.0053
- acc: 0.9998 - val_loss: 0.0793 - val_acc: 0.9860
Epoch 28/30
29409/29409 [==============================] - 115s 4ms/step - loss: 0.0051
- acc: 0.9998 - val_loss: 0.0794 - val_acc: 0.9862
Epoch 29/30
29409/29409 [==============================] - 114s 4ms/step - loss: 0.0050
- acc: 0.9998 - val_loss: 0.0795 - val_acc: 0.9864
Epoch 30/30
29409/29409 [==============================] - 113s 4ms/step - loss: 0.0048
- acc: 0.9998 - val_loss: 0.0796 - val_acc: 0.9865
```

After 30 epochs, the model is well trained, with 98.65% accuracy achieved on the testing set. In the RStudio viewer pane, we can also see the classification performance for each epoch in real time:

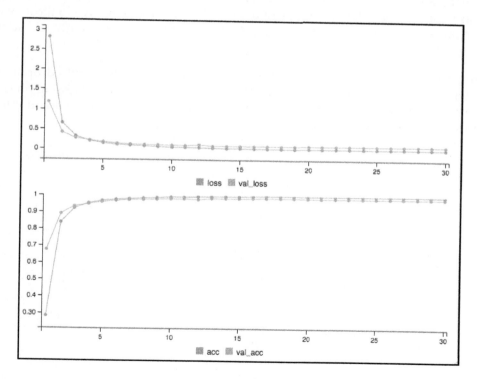

Reducing overfitting with dropout

You may notice that we had employed L2 regularization in the MXNet solution, which adds penalties for large weights in order to avoid overfitting; but we did not do so in this Keras solution. This results in a slight difference in classification accuracy on the testing set (99.30% versus 98.65%). We are going to employ regularization in our Keras solution, specifically **dropout** this time.

Dropout is a regularization technique in neural networks initially proposed by Geoffrey Hinton et. al. in 2012 (*Improving Neural Networks by Preventing Co-adaptation of Feature Detectors* in *Neural and Evolutionary Computing*). As the name implies, it ignores a small subset of neurons (can be hidden or visible) that are randomly selected in a neural network during training. The *dropped-out* neurons temporarily make no contribution to the activation of downstream neurons or the weight updates to neurons on backward pass. So how is the dropout technique able to prevent overfitting?

Recall that in a standard neural network, neurons are co-dependent among neighboring neurons during training. And weights of neurons are tuned for a particular context within the network, which restricts the individual power of each neuron. Such reliance on context may cause the model to be too specialized to training data. When some neurons in the network are not considered, the weights of neurons become less sensitive to those of other neurons. Neurons are forces to learn useful information more independently. Co-adaptation on training data is penalized.

Employing dropout is simple. During the training phase and in a layer with dropout rate p, for each iteration, we randomly switch off a fraction p of neurons. In the testing phase, we use all neurons but scale their activations by a factor of $q = 1 - p$, in order to account for the dropped-out activations in the training phase.

Here is a standard neural network (first image) and the same network with dropout (second image):

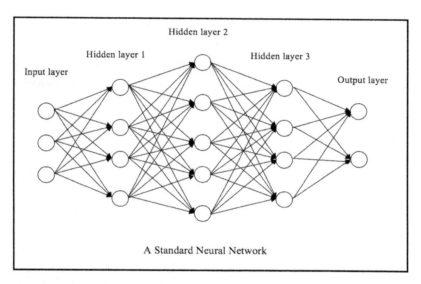

A Standard Neural Network

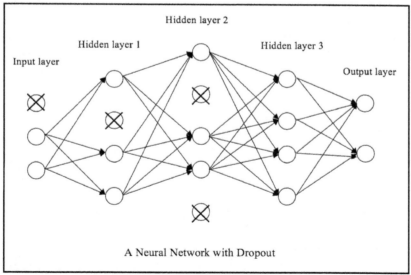

A Neural Network with Dropout

In this example, dropout is applied to a visible layer, the input layer, besides the hidden layers.

In practice, the dropout rate is usually set from 20% to 50%. A layer with a too low dropout rate makes little difference whereas a too high rate causes underfitting.

Now let's apply dropout to our Keras solution by using the function `layer_dropout(p)`. We define a function that initializes and compiles a CNN model with dropout (for reuse purposes):

```
> init_cnn_dropout <- function(){
+     model_dropout <- keras_model_sequential()
+     model_dropout %>%
+         layer_conv_2d(
+             filter = 32, kernel_size = c(5,5),
+             input_shape = c(32, 32, 1)
+         ) %>%
+         layer_activation("relu") %>%
+         layer_max_pooling_2d(pool_size = c(2,2)) %>%
+
+         # Second hidden convolutional layer layer
+         layer_conv_2d(filter = 64, kernel_size = c(5,5)) %>%
+         layer_activation("relu") %>%
+         # Use max pooling
+         layer_max_pooling_2d(pool_size = c(2,2)) %>%
+         layer_dropout(0.25) %>%
+
+         # Flatten and feed into dense layer
+         layer_flatten() %>%
+         layer_dense(1000) %>%
+         layer_activation("relu") %>%
+         layer_dropout(0.25) %>%
+
+         # Outputs from dense layer
+         layer_dense(43) %>%
+         layer_activation("softmax")
+
+     opt <- optimizer_sgd(lr = 0.005, momentum = 0.9)
+
+     model_dropout %>% compile(
+         loss = "categorical_crossentropy",
+         optimizer = opt,
+         metrics = "accuracy"
+     )
+     return(model_dropout)
+ }
```

Obtain a new model:

```
> model_dropout <- init_cnn_dropout()
```

We just employ 25% dropout in the second max pooling layer and 25% dropout in the fully connected hidden layer. By calling summary(model_dropout), we can see two dropout layers right below the second MaxPooling2D layer and the first dense and activation layer respectively.

Continue with the model training:

```
> model_dropout %>% fit(
+   x_train, y_train,
+   batch_size = 100,
+   epochs = 30,
+   validation_data = list(x_test, y_test),
+   shuffle = FALSE
+ )
Train on 29409 samples, validate on 9800 samples
Epoch 1/30
29409/29409 [==============================] - 108s 4ms/step - loss: 3.1078
- acc: 0.1987 - val_loss: 1.4475 - val_acc: 0.6487
Epoch 2/30
29409/29409 [==============================] - 106s 4ms/step - loss: 0.9772
- acc: 0.7337 - val_loss: 0.4570 - val_acc: 0.8934
Epoch 3/30
29409/29409 [==============================] - 106s 4ms/step - loss: 0.5194
- acc: 0.8598 - val_loss: 0.3043 - val_acc: 0.9310
Epoch 4/30
29409/29409 [==============================] - 106s 4ms/step - loss: 0.3606
- acc: 0.9037 - val_loss: 0.2058 - val_acc: 0.9529
Epoch 5/30
29409/29409 [==============================] - 106s 4ms/step - loss: 0.2828
- acc: 0.9250 - val_loss: 0.1677 - val_acc: 0.9640
Epoch 6/30
29409/29409 [==============================] - 106s 4ms/step - loss: 0.2272
- acc: 0.9406 - val_loss: 0.1424 - val_acc: 0.9707
Epoch 7/30
29409/29409 [==============================] - 106s 4ms/step - loss: 0.1910
- acc: 0.9494 - val_loss: 0.1138 - val_acc: 0.9793
Epoch 8/30
29409/29409 [==============================] - 106s 4ms/step - loss: 0.1560
- acc: 0.9602 - val_loss: 0.0986 - val_acc: 0.9797
Epoch 9/30
29409/29409 [==============================] - 106s 4ms/step - loss: 0.1423
- acc: 0.9621 - val_loss: 0.0956 - val_acc: 0.9804
Epoch 10/30
```

```
29409/29409 [==============================] - 106s 4ms/step - loss: 0.1256
- acc: 0.9663 - val_loss: 0.0814 - val_acc: 0.9841
Epoch 11/30
29409/29409 [==============================] - 106s 4ms/step - loss: 0.1111
- acc: 0.9708 - val_loss: 0.0760 - val_acc: 0.9847
Epoch 12/30
29409/29409 [==============================] - 106s 4ms/step - loss: 0.0987
- acc: 0.9735 - val_loss: 0.0795 - val_acc: 0.9824
Epoch 13/30
29409/29409 [==============================] - 106s 4ms/step - loss: 0.0899
- acc: 0.9752 - val_loss: 0.0626 - val_acc: 0.9876
Epoch 14/30
29409/29409 [==============================] - 106s 4ms/step - loss: 0.0799
- acc: 0.9787 - val_loss: 0.0665 - val_acc: 0.9868
Epoch 15/30
29409/29409 [==============================] - 106s 4ms/step - loss: 0.0794
- acc: 0.9792 - val_loss: 0.0571 - val_acc: 0.9887
Epoch 16/30
29409/29409 [==============================] - 106s 4ms/step - loss: 0.0691
- acc: 0.9817 - val_loss: 0.0534 - val_acc: 0.9898
Epoch 17/30
29409/29409 [==============================] - 106s 4ms/step - loss: 0.0668
- acc: 0.9817 - val_loss: 0.0560 - val_acc: 0.9892
Epoch 18/30
29409/29409 [==============================] - 106s 4ms/step - loss: 0.0583
- acc: 0.9846 - val_loss: 0.0486 - val_acc: 0.9916
Epoch 19/30
29409/29409 [==============================] - 106s 4ms/step - loss: 0.0541
- acc: 0.9861 - val_loss: 0.0484 - val_acc: 0.9914
Epoch 20/30
29409/29409 [==============================] - 106s 4ms/step - loss: 0.0529
- acc: 0.9858 - val_loss: 0.0494 - val_acc: 0.9906
Epoch 21/30
29409/29409 [==============================] - 106s 4ms/step - loss: 0.0500
- acc: 0.9864 - val_loss: 0.0449 - val_acc: 0.9909
Epoch 22/30
29409/29409 [==============================] - 106s 4ms/step - loss: 0.0469
- acc: 0.9872 - val_loss: 0.0414 - val_acc: 0.9926
Epoch 23/30
29409/29409 [==============================] - 106s 4ms/step - loss: 0.0473
- acc: 0.9863 - val_loss: 0.0415 - val_acc: 0.9917
Epoch 24/30
29409/29409 [==============================] - 107s 4ms/step - loss: 0.0406
- acc: 0.9894 - val_loss: 0.0416 - val_acc: 0.9916
Epoch 25/30
29409/29409 [==============================] - 108s 4ms/step - loss: 0.0413
- acc: 0.9888 - val_loss: 0.0445 - val_acc: 0.9909
Epoch 26/30
```

```
29409/29409 [==============================] - 108s 4ms/step - loss: 0.0337
- acc: 0.9906 - val_loss: 0.0412 - val_acc: 0.9922
Epoch 27/30
29409/29409 [==============================] - 108s 4ms/step - loss: 0.0333
- acc: 0.9911 - val_loss: 0.0388 - val_acc: 0.9928
Epoch 28/30
29409/29409 [==============================] - 108s 4ms/step - loss: 0.0332
- acc: 0.9905 - val_loss: 0.0395 - val_acc: 0.9933
Epoch 29/30
29409/29409 [==============================] - 108s 4ms/step - loss: 0.0312
- acc: 0.9910 - val_loss: 0.0371 - val_acc: 0.9937
Epoch 30/30
29409/29409 [==============================] - 108s 4ms/step - loss: 0.0305
- acc: 0.9917 - val_loss: 0.0383 - val_acc: 0.9940
```

With dropout, the prediction accuracy on the testing set is increased to 99.40%.

Dealing with a small training set – data augmentation

We have been very fortunate so far to possess a large-enough training dataset with 75% of 39,209 samples. This is one of the reasons why we are able to achieve a 99.3% to 99.4% classification accuracy. However, in reality, obtaining a large training set is not easy in most supervised learning cases, where manual work is necessary or the cost of data collection and labeling is high. In our traffic signs classification project, can we still achieve the same performance if we are given a lot less training samples to begin with? Let's give it a shot.

We simulate a small training set with only 10% of the 39,209 samples and a testing set with the rest 90%:

```
> train_perc_1 = 0.1
> train_index_1 <- createDataPartition(data.y, p=train_perc_1, list=FALSE)
> train_index_1 <- train_index_1[sample(nrow(train_index_1)),]
> data_train_1.x <- data.x[train_index_1,]
> data_train_1.y <- data.y[train_index_1]
> data_test_1.x <- data.x[-train_index_1,]
> data_test_1.y <- data.y[-train_index_1]
> x_train_1 <- data_train_1.x
> dim(x_train_1) <- c(nrow(data_train_1.x), 32, 32, 1)
> x_test_1 <- data_test_1.x
> dim(x_test_1) <- c(nrow(data_test_1.x), 32, 32, 1)
> y_train_1 <- to_categorical(data_train_1.y, num_classes = 43)
> y_test_1 <- to_categorical(data_test_1.y, num_classes = 43)
```

Initialize a new model and fit it with the new training set:

```
> model_1 <- init_cnn_dropout()
> model_1 %>% fit(
+    x_train_1, y_train_1,
+    batch_size = 100,
+    epochs = 1,
+    validation_data = list(x_test_1, y_test_1),
+    shuffle = FALSE
+ )
```

Train on 3,921 samples; validate on 35,288 samples:

```
Epoch 1/30
3921/3921 [==============================] - 19s 5ms/step - loss: 3.6705 -
acc: 0.0594 - val_loss: 3.5191 - val_acc: 0.0592
Epoch 2/30
3921/3921 [==============================] - 17s 4ms/step - loss: 3.5079 -
acc: 0.0681 - val_loss: 3.4663 - val_acc: 0.0529
......
......
Epoch 29/30
3921/3921 [==============================] - 17s 4ms/step - loss: 0.1935 -
acc: 0.9462 - val_loss: 0.2760 - val_acc: 0.9381
Epoch 30/30
3921/3921 [==============================] - 17s 4ms/step - loss: 0.1962 -
acc: 0.9431 - val_loss: 0.2772 - val_acc: 0.9393
```

It is not bad to achieve 93.93% accuracy by a model trained with only 3,921 samples. But can we do better, at least close to 99% as we accomplished with sufficient training data? Yes! One solution is data augmentation.

Data augmentation simply means expanding the size of the existing data that we feed to the supervised learning models in order to compensate for the cost of further data collection and labeling.

There are many ways to augment data in computer vision. The simplest one is probably flipping an image horizontally or vertically. Take the General caution sign as an example; we implement flipping using the function flow_images_from_data() in Keras as follows.

Load the General caution sample:

```
> img<-image_load(paste(training_path, "00018/00001_00004.ppm", sep=""))
> img1<-image_to_array(img)
> dim(img1)<-c(1,dim(img1))
```

We generate a horizontally flipped image and save the resulting image in the `augmented` directory we created:

```
> images_iter  <- flow_images_from_data(img1, , generator =
                image_data_generator(horizontal_flip = TRUE),
+               save_to_dir = 'augmented',
+               save_prefix = "horizontal", save_format = "png")
> reticulate::iter_next(images_iter)
```

The flipped sign (right) along with the original image (left) is displayed as follows:

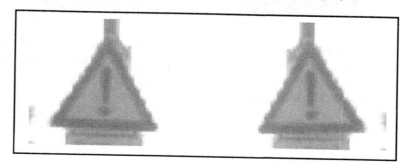

The horizontally flipped sign image conveys the same message as the original one. It should be noted that flipping works only in orientation-insensitive cases, such as a classification between cats and dogs, or our recognition of traffic lights. However, in cases where orientation matters, such as a classification between right turn and left turn, a small to medium degree rotation can still be applied. For instance, flipping the *Dangerous curve to the right* sign is absolutely dangerous, but rotating it by at most 20 degrees is harmless and even helpful, as we can see in the following example:

```
> img<-image_load(paste(training_path, "00020/00002_00017.ppm", sep=""))
> img1<-image_to_array(img)
> dim(img1)<-c(1,dim(img1))
> images_iter  <- flow_images_from_data(img1, , generator =
                image_data_generator(rotation_range = 20),
+               save_to_dir = 'augmented',
+               save_prefix = "rotation", save_format = "png")
> reticulate::iter_next(images_iter)
```

The rotated sign (right) and the original image (left) contain identical information:

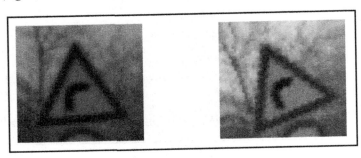

Shifting is perhaps the most common augmentation method. Moving the image horizontally and/or vertically by a small number of pixels generates an identically functioning image. Using the same example as before, we shift it horizontally and vertically by at most 20% of the width and height:

```
> images_iter  <- flow_images_from_data(img1,
            generator=image_data_generator(width_shift_range=0.2,
            height_shift_range=0.2), save_to_dir = 'augmented',
+           save_prefix = "shift", save_format = "png")
> reticulate::iter_next(images_iter)
```

This results in a shifted image in the right half here:

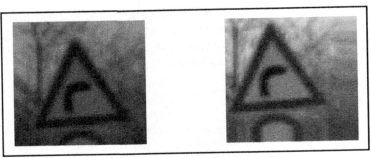

Armed with common augmentation approaches, let's augment our small training dataset by at most 20 degrees' rotation and at most 20% shifting (note that we cannot apply flipping as some signs, such as class 19, 20, 21, 33, and 34, are not semantically symmetric):

```
> datagen <- image_data_generator(
+    rotation_range = 20,
+    width_shift_range = 0.2,
+    height_shift_range = 0.2,
+    horizontal_flip = FALSE
+ )
>
> datagen %>% fit_image_data_generator(x_train_1)
Augmented data generator is defined and now being applied to a CNN model
with function fit_generator:
> model_2 <- init_cnn_dropout()
> model_2 %>% fit_generator(
+    flow_images_from_data(x_train_1, y_train_1,
                           datagen, batch_size = 100),
+    steps_per_epoch = as.integer(50000/100),
+    epochs = 30,
+    validation_data = list(x_test_1, y_test_1)
+ )
Epoch 1/30
500/500 [==============================] - 74s 149ms/step - loss: 3.4566 -
acc: 0.0798 - val_loss: 3.2963 - val_acc: 0.1322
Epoch 2/30
500/500 [==============================] - 77s 153ms/step - loss: 3.0920 -
acc: 0.1666 - val_loss: 2.1010 - val_acc: 0.4249
......
......
Epoch 25/30
500/500 [==============================] - 83s 166ms/step - loss: 0.1396 -
acc: 0.9584 - val_loss: 0.0636 - val_acc: 0.9860
Epoch 26/30
500/500 [==============================] - 79s 158ms/step - loss: 0.1359 -
acc: 0.9592 - val_loss: 0.0672 - val_acc: 0.9859
Epoch 27/30
500/500 [==============================] - 80s 160ms/step - loss: 0.1344 -
acc: 0.9600 - val_loss: 0.0727 - val_acc: 0.9843
Epoch 28/30
500/500 [==============================] - 81s 163ms/step - loss: 0.1227 -
acc: 0.9628 - val_loss: 0.0647 - val_acc: 0.9862
Epoch 29/30
500/500 [==============================] - 79s 158ms/step - loss:
```

```
0.1222 - acc: 0.9627 - val_loss: 0.0668 - val_acc: 0.9858
Epoch 30/30
500/500 [==============================] - 80s 160ms/step - loss: 0.1220 -
acc: 0.9636 - val_loss: 0.0614 - val_acc: 0.9870
```

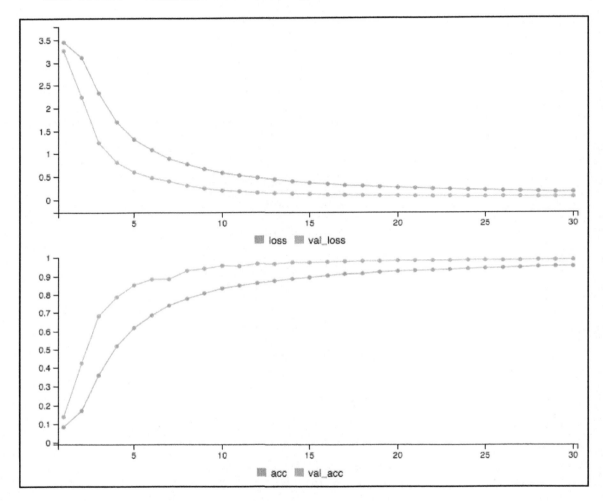

With data augmentation, we can get excellent results of 98.70% accuracy with a small training set.

Besides the 4.77% (93.93% to 98.70%) performance increase compared to no data augmentation, we observe that each iteration takes a longer time than before (around 20 s to around 80 s). This is because `image_data_generator()` generates mini-batches of augmented image data in real time for each iteration. So, even if the same set of samples is used in two iterations, the augmented data can be very different. Such setting adds more variation to the training set, which in turn makes the model more robust. And that is why data augmentation is considered an approach to reduce overfitting.

Another particularly useful application of data augmentation is balancing a dataset. In most unbalanced classification cases (such as online ads click-through prediction, or banking fraud detection), we usually down-sample the dominant class. However, this can be counterproductive for small datasets. The alternative solution is to augment data from the minor class.

Last but not least, there are other approaches not mentioned previously to augment image data. For example, rescaling multiplies pixel values by a factor and, as a result, changes the lighting condition. Shearing and zooming are useful data augmentation transformations as well. They can be specified in `image_data_generator()`. If interested, you can try applying any of these approaches and see whether you can beat 98.70%.

Reviewing methods to prevent overfitting in CNNs

Overfitting occurs when the model fits too well to the training set but is not able to generalize to unseen cases. For example, a CNN model recognizes specific traffic sign images in the training set instead of general patterns. It can be very dangerous if a self-driving car is not able to recognize sign images in ever-changing conditions, such as different weather, lighting, and angles different from what are presented in the training set. To recap, here's what we can do to reduce overfitting:

- Collecting more training data (if possible and feasible) in order to account for various input data.
- Using data augmentation, wherein we *invent* data in a smart way if time or cost does not allow us to collect more data.
- Employing dropout, which diminishes complex co-adaptations among neighboring neurons.

- Adding Lasso (L1) or/and Ridge (L2) penalty, which prevents model coefficients from fitting so perfectly that overfitting arises.
- Reducing the complexity of network architecture. Recall that in the last chapter, we mentioned that adding hidden layers will not help boost the model performance but increase chances of overfitting.

Summary

We just accomplished our second computer vision project in this R and deep learning journey! Through this chapter, we got more familiar with convolutional neural networks and their implementation in MXNet, and another powerful deep learning tool: Keras with TensorFlow.

We started with what self-driving cars are and how deep learning techniques are making self-driving cars feasible and more reliable. We also discussed how deep learning stands out and becomes the state-of-the-art solution for object recognition in intelligent vehicles. After exploring the traffic sign dataset, we developed our first CNN model using MXNet and achieved more than 99% accuracy. Then we moved on to another powerful deep learning framework, Keras + TensorFlow, and obtained comparable results.

We introduced the dropout technique to reduce overfitting. We also learned how to deal with lack of training data and utilize data augmentation techniques, including flipping, shifting, and rotation. We finally wrapped up the chapter by summarizing some approaches to prevent overfitting in CNN models. That was the second example where we observed how deep learning removes manual or explicit feature extraction steps taken in traditional approaches, and instead efficiently finds the best sets of features.

We have practiced CNNs in these two computer vision projects. In the next project, we will be working with totally different types of deep neural networks—autoencoders.

3
Fraud Detection with Autoencoders

In this chapter, we continue our journey into deep learning with R with **autoencoders**.

A classical autoencoder consists of three parts:

- **An encoding function**, which compresses your data
- **A decoding function**, which reconstructs data from a compressed version
- **A metric or distance**, which calculates the difference between the information lost by compression on your data

We typically assume that all these involved functions are smooth enough to be able to use backpropagation or other gradient-based methods, although they need not be and we could use derivative-free methods to train them.

 Autoencoding is the process of summarizing information from a potentially large feature set into a smaller feature set.

Although the compression bit might remind you of algorithms, such as the MP3 compression algorithm, an important difference is that autoencoders are data specific. An autoencoder trained in pictures of cats and dogs will likely perform poorly in pictures of buildings. In contrast, the MP3 compression algorithm uses assumptions of sound in general and can work regardless of the sound data. The data-specific bit is a serious caveat for widespread application which makes autoencoders rarely used for compression tasks.

One reason autoencoders have attracted so much attention in recent years is because many people believe that they might be the key for **unsupervised learning,** although strictly speaking, they are a **self-supervised** learning algorithm.

Sometimes the features abstracted from autoencoders can be fed into supervised learning algorithms, making them somewhat comparable to **principal component analysis (PCA)** as a dimensionality reduction technique.

Autoencoders are typically used in computer vision problems such as image denoising or for picking up features such as colors, light and edges. They are also used for data visualization of large dimensional datasets, as they can find more interesting features than PCA. Other recent applications include fraud and intrusion detection.

For our purposes, an autoencoder neural network is simply an algorithm for unsupervised learning that applies backpropagation by setting the target values equal to the inputs, if $x_1, x_2, ... x_m$ are the training examples and $y_1, y_2, ... y_m$ are the labels, then we will do backpropagation by setting $x_i = y_i$ for all values of i.

From your previous experience with machine learning, you might be familiar with PCA. Don't worry if you are not familiar with it, this is not strictly required for our purposes. PCA is a **dimensionality reduction** technique, which means, given a set of training examples, a suitable transformation is applied (for math geeks, this is just a projection into the vector space generated by the eigenvectors of the covariance matrix). The goal of this projection is to find the most relevant features of the input data, so that in the end we get a simplified representation of it.

Autoencoders work in a similar vein, except that the transformation involved is not a projection, but rather a non-linear function f. Given a training example x, an autoencoder encodes x using a neural network into a hidden state $h:=f(x)$, and decodes h using a function g, which brings an overall transformation of $x => g(f(x))$. If the result of this process would be simply $g(f(x))=x$, we would not have a very useful transformation. The idea is illustrated in the following diagram:

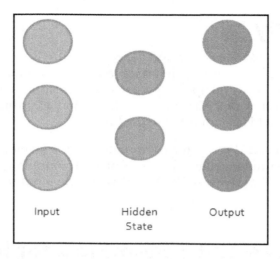

A simple autoencoder in action: Encoding a three-dimensional vector into a two-dimensional hidden state, and then back to a three-dimensional space.

On the left part, a three-dimensional input vector is transformed into a two-dimensional encoded state (this is the action of *f*) and then transformed back into a three-dimensional vector (by the action of *g*).

Why do we take the trouble of encoding and decoding? This has two purposes. On one hand, autoencoders provide, as PCA, a way to automatically generate features in a lower dimensional space. This is useful as part of a machine learning pipeline for **feature extraction**, in the same way PCA is also useful. Synthesizing the data and automatically generating features (instead of relying on domain expertise and feature handcrafting) to improve the accuracy of a supervised learning algorithm, be it for classification or regression tasks. For our purposes, it is also useful for outlier detection. As the computer is forced to understand the essential features of the data, anything that jumps out as odd will be thrown away during the reconstruction process (that is, the full encoding–decoding cycle), and the outliers will be easily identifiable.

Before jumping into the fraud example for this chapter, let's get our feet wet looking at a simpler example, and at the same time getting our tools ready.

Getting ready

In this chapter, we will introduce `keras` and `tensorflow` for R. `keras` is a model-level building, in that it provides a high-level interface to quickly develop deep learning models. Instead of implementing low-level operations such as convolutions and tensor products, it relies on Theano, TensorFlow or CNTK in the backend, and according to the development team, more backends would be supported in the future.

Why do you need a backend? Well, if the computation becomes more complicated, which is often the case in deep learning, you need to use different computation methods (known as computation graphs) and hardware (GPUs). For instructional purposes, all our sample codes run without GPU.

Installing Keras and TensorFlow for R

As per the official documentation, you can install Keras simply with:

```
devtools::install_github("rstudio/keras")
```

The Keras R interface uses `tensorflow` as a backend engine by default. To install both the core `keras` library and `tensorflow`, then do:

```
library(keras)
install_keras()
```

However smooth this might seem, we have seen this setup fail a number of times. Our recommended plan B is:

- Download and install the Anaconda distribution for Python. This is the standard data science stack, with the most popular Python libraries for data scientists.
- Install your Keras backend, for instance, Tensorflow.
- Install Keras (within Python).

After this, you should be ready to install Keras in R.

To be sure that you are working with the most recent version of R, you can update it from R GUI (not from RStudio) using the `installr` package:

```
### Run these from RGUi
 install.packages("installr")
 installr::updateR()
```

Once you are done, you can install `keras` with `devtools`:

```
install.packages("devtools")
devtools::install_github("rstudio/keras")
```

Finally, check that everything is correct by importing the library:

```
library(keras)
```

The preceding instructions worked well for a laptop with Windows 10, running R version 3.4. If you have an older version and you do not want to update, you need to install the dependencies specified as follows (I tried this with R version 3.3):

```
install.packages("Rcpp")
install.packages("devtools")
devtools::install_github("rstudio/reticulate", force=TRUE)
devtools::install_github("r-lib/debugme")
devtools::install_github("r-lib/processx")
devtools::install_github("tidyverse/rlang")
devtools::install_github("tidyverse/glue")
devtools::install_github("tidyverse/tidyselect")
devtools::install_github("rstudio/tfruns")
devtools::install_github("rstudio/tensorflow")
devtools::install_github("rstudio/keras")
devtools::install_github("jeroen/jsonlite")
```

Installing H2O

We will also show you how to use H2O for some of the exercises. The easiest way to install H2O is to get it from CRAN.

It has a few dependencies, notably the packages:

- `RCurl`
- `bitops`
- `rjson`
- `statmod`
- `tools`

If you run into trouble, chances are that there is some dependency missing. Re-read the error message and install any missing packages.

If it all goes smoothly, import the library and initialize the service to check that everything works:

```
install.packages("h2o")
library(h2o)
h2o.init()
```

Our first examples

Let's begin with a few simple examples to understand what is going on.

For some of us, it's very easy to get tempted to try the shiniest algorithms and do hyper-parameter optimization instead of the less glamorous step-by-step understanding.

A simple 2D example

Let's develop our intuition of how the autoencoder works with a simple two-dimensional example.

We first generate 10,000 points coming from a normal distribution with mean 0 and variance 1:

```
library(MASS)
library(keras)
Sigma <- matrix(c(1,0,0,1),2,2)
n_points <- 10000
df <- mvrnorm(n=n_points, rep(0,2), Sigma)
df <- as.data.frame(df)
```

The distribution of the values should look as follows:

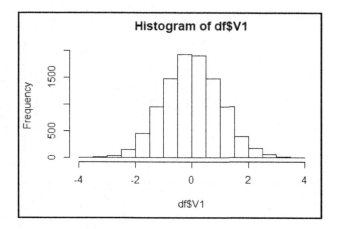

Distribution of the variable V1 we just generated; the variable V2 looks fairly similar.

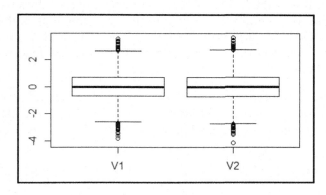

Distribution of the variables V1 and V2 we generated.

Let's spice things up a bit and add some outliers to the mixture. In many fraud applications, the fraud rate is about 1–5%, so we generate 1% of our samples as coming from a normal distribution, with mean 5 and standard deviation 1:

```
# Set the outliers
n_outliers <- as.integer(0.01*n_points)
idxs <- sample(n_points, size = n_outliers)
outliers <- mvrnorm(n=n_outliers, rep(5,2), Sigma)
df[idxs,] <- outliers
```

The new distribution of points looks like this now:

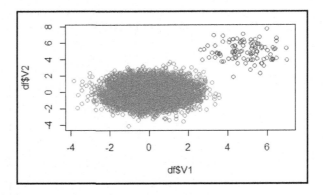

New distribution of points after adding the outliers.

We will use an autoencoder with a single neural network in the hidden layer. Why not add more? The problem is that if the hidden state has equal or higher dimensions than the input state, we risk that our model might learn the identity function, that is, that the model learns $g(f(x))=x$ everywhere. This is clearly not a very useful outlier identification method. We need to capture the essential features of the data, so that those unusual features would be highlighted later on, hence allowing to detect outliers.

With `keras`, it is really easy to set up the model, we need an input layer of shape 2, for our two-dimensional example. This is passed to our one-dimensional encoder, using a ReLU activation function and then decoded back into a two-dimensional space:

```
input_layer <- layer_input(shape=c(2))
 encoder <- layer_dense(units=1, activation='relu')(input_layer)
 decoder <- layer_dense(units=2)(encoder)
 autoencoder <- keras_model(inputs=input_layer, outputs = decoder)
```

Before using the model, we need to compile it. We need to specify a loss functional, a metric to optimize and an algorithm to perform the gradient descent updates. We will go for the Adam solver, optimizing the classical mean squared error (that works in this problem, but we might need to change it for our particular application) and choose accuracy as the metric to optimize:

```
autoencoder %>% compile(optimizer='adam',
loss='mean_squared_error',
metrics=c('accuracy'))
```

Once this is set up, we are ready for training:

```
# Coerce the dataframe to matrix to perform the training
df <- as.matrix(df)
history <- autoencoder %>% fit(
df, df,
epochs = 30, batch_size = 128,
validation_split = 0.2
)
```

Using the command, `plot(history)`, we can see how the training went for this example:

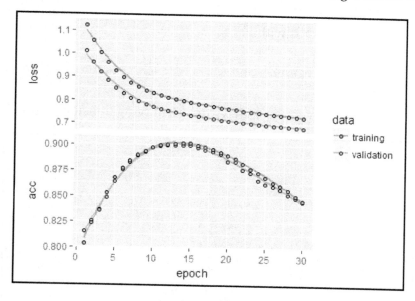

Training of our autoencoder.

So we see that, while the accuracy remains fairly high, there is a mysterious drop during the training. We should not worry too much about it for now, we will come to this issue later. As for the loss, it keeps decreasing as we add more data, which is expected.

Finally, Let's look at the reconstruction. We first generate the predictions from our trained autoencoder:

```
preds <- autoencoder %>% predict(df)
colnames(preds) <- c("V1", "V2")
preds <- as.data.frame(preds)
```

This is the reconstruction of the points, as per our autoencoder. We will color red those points whose reconstruction is at a (Euclidean) distance larger than three from the original images, and leave the others blue. Why those points? Our autoencoder learned that our dataset had some intrinsic properties (it learned the distribution of the average point), so in those points where the reconstruction error is anomalously large, there might be something worth looking at:

```
# Coerce back the matrix to data frame to use ggplot later
df <- as.data.frame(df)
# Euclidean distance larger than 3 = sum of squares larger than 9
df$color <- ifelse((df$V1-preds$V1)**2+(df$V2-preds$V2)**2>9,"red","blue")
```

Finally, we can look at the results with `ggplot`:

```
library(ggplot2)
 df %>% ggplot(aes(V1,V2),col=df$color)+geom_point(color = df$color,
position="jitter")
```

The following screenshot shows how well we did identifying unusual points:

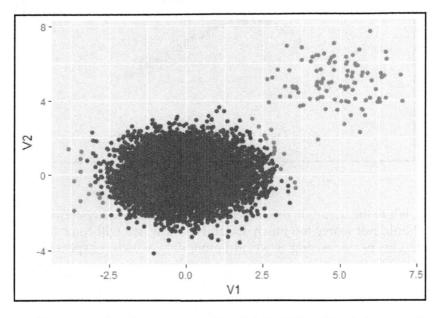

Output of the autoencoder. In blue. the reconstructed points by our autoencoder. In red, the original points in the dataset. We see that there is a cloud of red points that thanks to our autoencoder we can identify as unusual.

In the preceding screenshot, the blue points are the reconstructed images from the autoencoder. We see that it learned correctly that most of the points come from a normal distribution centered at *(0,0)*, as expected. However there are still some points which are *normal* on the original dataset and where pointed out as unusual. No need to get discouraged from learning autoencoders that soon, the reason for this is that the autoencoder we used is rather simple. We will look at more sophisticated ways to tackle the outlier detection problem with autoencoders.

Autoencoders and MNIST

Many examples of deep learning algorithms in either research papers, blog posts or books deal with the MNIST dataset. We should not be the exception and introduce a small use case for autoencoders using MNIST.

The motivation is the following, suppose you want to detect fake banknotes automatically. Then you would need to teach the computer what the representation of the *average banknote* is to be able to detect those that have significant differences. Due to the large volume of cash transactions happening every day worldwide, and to the increasing sophistication of fraudsters, it would be unthinkable to do this process manually. One way to do this is to use sophisticated imaging software, which is how counterfeit banknote detectors, such as D40 or D50, work.

Another reason for using MNIST is obviously practical. At the time of writing I was unable to find a nice training dataset with counterfeit banknotes, and MNIST comes already preinstalled in `keras`.

We start with loading the dataset:

```
library(keras)
mnist <- dataset_mnist()
X_train <- mnist$train$x
y_train <- mnist$train$y
X_test <- mnist$test$x
y_test <- mnist$test$y
```

Let's take a closer look at the dataset:

```
image(X_train[1,,], col=gray.colors(3))
y_train[1]
```

If everything works correctly, you should see the image of the number five.

We need to do a bit of preprocessing before training our autoencoder. The X_train data is a three-dimensional array (images, width, height) of grayscale values. We need to first convert these arrays into matrices by reshaping the height and width into a single vector, so that instead of dealing with 28 x 28 squares we have a *28*28=784* vector. Then, we convert the grayscale values from integers ranging between 0 to 255 into floating point values, ranging between 0 and 1:

```
# reshape
dim(X_train) <- c(nrow(X_train), 784)
dim(X_test) <- c(nrow(X_test), 784)
# rescale
X_train <- X_train / 255
X_test <- X_test / 255
```

Once the initial preprocessing is done, we define the topology of our autoencoder. Let's use an encoding layer with 32 neurons, to achieve a compression ratio of *784/32 = 24.5*:

```
input_dim <- 28*28 #784
inner_layer_dim <- 32
input_layer <- layer_input(shape=c(input_dim))
encoder <- layer_dense(units=inner_layer_dim,
activation='relu')(input_layer)
decoder <- layer_dense(units=784)(encoder)
autoencoder <- keras_model(inputs=input_layer, outputs = decoder)
```

We are ready to compile and train the model:

```
autoencoder %>% compile(optimizer='adam',
 loss='mean_squared_error',
 metrics=c('accuracy'))
history <- autoencoder %>% fit(
 X_train,X_train,
 epochs = 50, batch_size = 256,
 validation_split=0.2
 )
```

Using the plot command, we can see the performance of our model during the training and validation as follows:

```
plot(history)
```

Even better, if you are using RStudio as your IDE, there is a real-time view in the **Viewer** panel. With this command you should see two plots, showing the accuracy and loss as a function of the epoch number:

Use the **Viewer** panel to see the training in real time. Click on the **Open in New Window** button:

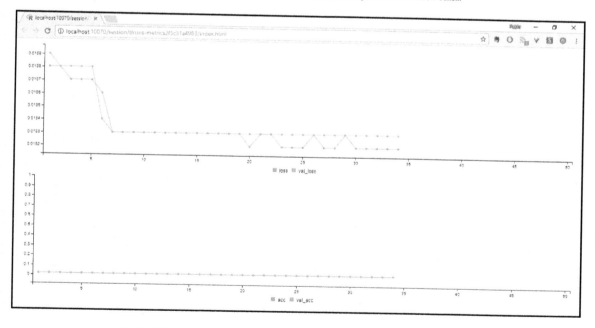

Real time training. On the horizontal axis, the epoch number. Loss and accuracy are shown in the vertical axes.

Using the `predict` method, we reconstruct the digits and compute the reconstruction errors:

```
# Reconstruct on the test set
preds <- autoencoder %>% predict(X_test)
error <- rowSums((preds-X_test)**2)
error
```

Intuitively, some classes might be harder to predict, because some people write numbers in slightly different ways. Which classes have a higher reconstruction error?

```
# Which were more problematic to reconstruct?
eval <- data.frame(error=error, class=as.factor(y_test))
library(dplyr)
eval %>% group_by(class) %>% summarise(avg_error=mean(error))

## OUTPUT
# A tibble: 10 x 2
   class avg_error
   <fctr> <dbl>
 1 0 14.091963
 2 1 6.126858
 3 2 17.245944
 4 3 14.138960
 5 4 13.189842
 6 5 15.170581
 7 6 14.570642
 8 7 11.778826
 9 8 16.120203
10 9 11.645038
```

Note that, some small variations are expected, since there is, for instance, a random component involved in the shuffling of the data. However, the general trends should be similar.

An image says more than a thousand words, so even better than summarizing our data with `dplyr`, we can use `ggplot2` to visualize this information:

```
library(ggplot2)
eval %>%
  group_by(class) %>%
  summarise(avg_error=mean(error)) %>%
  ggplot(aes(x=class,fill=class,y=avg_error))+geom_col()
```

We can see, as follows, how our reconstruction error performed per class. This is important as it will let's know if our classifier is biased in some way, or if it finds some classes harder to train than others:

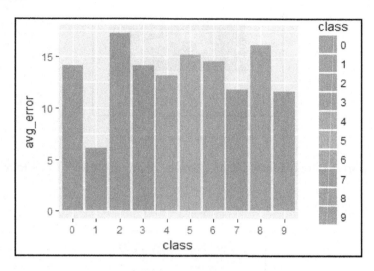

Reconstruction error in the MNIST dataset. 2 and 8 seem to be the most problematic classes, and 1 seems the most straight forward to recognize.

Well, that is certainly useful and interesting to see, we see that **2** is somewhat harder to reconstruct, which might be due to the fact that it looks like a **7** sometimes. Intuitively, **8** could be easily confused with **9** or with **0**, so the results somehow make sense.

An even better way to look at how our reconstruction autoencoder is performing, is to look directly at the reconstructed examples. For this, we need first to reshape back our original data and the reconstruction:

```
# Reshape original and reconstructed
dim(X_test) <- c(nrow(X_test),28,28)
dim(preds) <- c(nrow(preds),28,28)
```

And now let's look at the reconstructed image:

```
image(255*preds[1,,], col=gray.colors(3))
```

Let's look at the reconstructed image of a typical element of the test set:

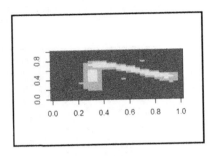

Reconstructed image by our autoencoder.

How does it compare to the original image, before reconstruction? Let's take a look:

```
y_test[1]
    image(255*X_test[1,,], col=gray.colors(3))
```

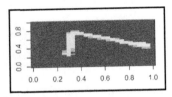

Original image.

Overall, not bad for a 24.5 compression! Clearly there is a lot to be improved, but we can already see the potential of autoencoders to learn intrinsic features of the data.

Outlier detection in MNIST

All right, so admittedly our previous application has nothing to do with fraud or outlier detection so far. We can do a small modification on the previous setup to show how a similar framework works. For this, let's assume that the number 7 is an outlier class and we will try to identify it from the result of our *normal* numbers: 0, 1, 2 , 3, 4, 5, 6, 8, 9.

We will train the autoencoder on the *normal* dataset and then apply it to the test set. The aim will be to abstract as many features of the *normal* situation as possible. This requires knowledge of the *normal* situation, which translates into availability of labelled data and hence, it is an ideal scenario, for many practical applications, for instance credit card fraud or intrusion detection, we sometimes (or rather often) lack such labeled data.

We begin as before:

```
library(keras)
mnist <- dataset_mnist()
X_train <- mnist$train$x
y_train <- mnist$train$y
X_test <- mnist$test$x
y_test <- mnist$test$y
```

But now we will exclude 7 from the training set, as it will be the outlier in our example.

```
## Exclude "7" from the training set. "7" will be the outlier
outlier_idxs <- which(y_train!=7, arr.ind = T)
X_train <- X_train[outlier_idxs,,]
y_test <- sapply(y_test, function(x){ ifelse(x==7,"outlier","normal")})
```

We continue as before, with re-scaling and reshaping before defining our autoencoder:

```
# reshape
dim(X_train) <- c(nrow(X_train), 784)
dim(X_test) <- c(nrow(X_test), 784)
# rescale
X_train <- X_train / 255
X_test <- X_test / 255
input_dim <- 28*28 #784
inner_layer_dim <- 32
# Create the autoencoder
input_layer <- layer_input(shape=c(input_dim))
encoder <- layer_dense(units=inner_layer_dim,
activation='relu')(input_layer)
decoder <- layer_dense(units=784)(encoder)
autoencoder <- keras_model(inputs=input_layer, outputs = decoder)
autoencoder %>% compile(optimizer='adam',
                        loss='mean_squared_error',
                        metrics=c('accuracy'))
history <- autoencoder %>% fit(
 X_train,X_train,
 epochs = 50, batch_size = 256,
 validation_split=0.2
)
plot(history)
```

Once the autoencoder is trained, we can start looking at the performance, using the reconstruction of the test set:

```
# Reconstruct on the test set
preds <- autoencoder %>% predict(X_test)
error <- rowSums((preds-X_test)**2)
eval <- data.frame(error=error, class=as.factor(y_test))
library(ggplot2)
library(dplyr)
eval %>%
  group_by(class) %>%
  summarise(avg_error=mean(error)) %>%
  ggplot(aes(x=class,fill=class,y=avg_error))+geom_boxplot()
```

Let's look at the reconstruction error in our different classes:

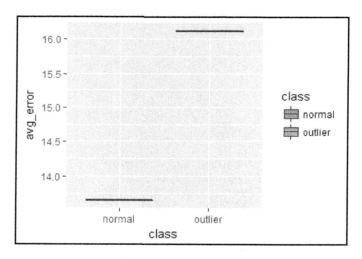

Distribution of reconstruction error in the test set

From the plot, we see that we can set up the threshold value at 15, that is, observations with a reconstruction error above 15 would be marked as outliers:

```
threshold <- 15
y_preds <- sapply(error, function(x)
ifelse(x>threshold, "outlier", "normal")})
```

Once this is done, we can calculate the confusion matrix. This is a useful way of visualizing what the model is doing:

```
# Confusion matrix
table(y_preds,y_test)
```

This gives us the following:

```
         y_test
y_preds   normal   outlier
  normal    5707       496
 outlier    3265       532
```

So clearly we could do better. Perhaps the vertical stroke shared by digits 1 and 7 contributes to the huge error rate. We caught, however, a bit over 50% of the outlier cases with this simple architecture. One way to improve this would be to add more hidden layers. We will use this trick later in this chapter.

Credit card fraud detection with autoencoders

Fraud is a multi-billion dollar industry, with credit card fraud being probably the closest to our daily lives. Fraud begins with the theft of the physical credit card or with data that could compromise the security of the account, such as the credit card number, expiration date and security codes. A stolen card can be reported directly, if the victim knows that their card has been stolen, however, when the data is stolen, a compromised account can take weeks or even months to be used, and the victim then only knows from their bank statement that the card has been used.

Traditionally, fraud detection systems rely on the creation of manually engineered features by subject matter experts, working either directly with financial institutions or with specialized software vendors.

One of the biggest challenges in fraud detection is the availability of labelled datasets, which are often hard or even impossible to come by.

Our first fraud example comes from a dataset made public in Kaggle, (`https://www.kaggle.com/dalpozz/creditcardfraud`), by researchers from the Université Libre de Bruxelles in Belgium (for the full work, you can read their paper: Andrea Dal Pozzolo, Olivier Caelen, Reid A. Johnson and Gianluca Bontempi, *Calibrating Probability with Undersampling for Unbalanced Classification. In Symposium on Computational Intelligence and Data Mining (CIDM), IEEE, 2015*).

The datasets contain transactions made by credit cards in two days in September 2013 by European cardholders. We have 492 frauds out of 284,807 transactions. Unlike toy datasets (I am looking at you, Iris), real-life datasets are highly unbalanced. In this example, the positive class (frauds) account for 0.172% of all transactions.

It contains just numerical information factors which are the aftereffect of a PCA change. Because of classification issues, the creators can't give the first highlights and more foundation data about the information. Features V1, V2, ... V28 are the chief segments got with PCA, the main features which have not been changed with PCA are `Time` and `Amount`.

The feature, `Time` contains the seconds elapsed between each transaction and the first transaction in the dataset. The feature, `Amount` is the transaction's amount, this feature can be used for example-dependent, cost-sensitive learning. The feature, `Class` is the response variable and it takes value 1 in case of fraud and 0 otherwise. Given the class imbalance ratio, the authors recommend measuring the area under the **precision-recall curve (AUC)**, instead of the confusion matrix. The precision-recall curve is also called **ROC** (receiver-operator characteristic).

At this point you might be thinking: well, why should I bother with autoencoders since this is clearly a binary classification problem, and we already have the labeled data? Sure, you can go the traditional way and try to do standard supervised learning algorithms, such as random forests or support vector machines, just be careful to either oversample the fraud class or undersample the normal class, so that these methods can perform well. However, in many real-life instances we do not have the labeled data beforehand, and in complex fraud scenarios it might be very tricky to get an accurate label. Suppose you are a criminal willing to commit fraud.

Previous to the fraud (or even after) you may have completely normal activity in your account. So shall we flag all of your transactions as rogue? Or only a certain subset? Some people in the business may argue that, after all, the transactions were committed by a criminal, so they are tainted somehow and we should flag all your activity, introducing bias into the model. Instead of relying on the label, we will treat the problem as an *anomaly detection* or *outlier detection* problem and use autoencoders, as before.

Exploratory data analysis

An often overlooked step is exploratory data analysis. Before jumping straight into the data and trying to do fancy deep learning architectures, let's step back and look at what we have around.

Let's begin by downloading the dataset from Kaggle: (`https://www.kaggle.com/dalpozz/creditcardfraud`) and importing it into R:

```
df <- read.csv("./data/creditcard.csv", stringsAsFactors = F)
head(df)
```

Before moving on, we should do a basic sanity check. Some of the things we should look for are:

- Verify that there are indeed only two classes (0 for normal transactions, 1 for fraudulent)
- Verify that the timestamp corresponds to two days
- Check that there are no missing values

Once this is done, we can perform two quick checks, an idea would be to see if there is an obvious pattern between the time of day and the amount. Perhaps fraudulent transactions happen at a certain time, when our system is vulnerable? We should check this first:

```
library(ggplot2)
library(dplyr)
 df %>% ggplot(aes(Time,Amount))+geom_point()+facet_grid(Class~.)
```

First, let's see if there is some seasonality pattern. We just plot the time variable against the amount, per class:

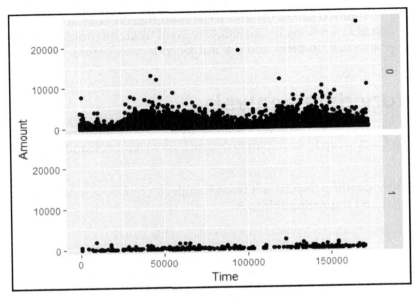

Quick inspection for fraud: the class 0 corresponds to normal transactions and the class 1 to fraudulent transactions.

So nothing jumps out. Interestingly, the amount involved in fraud transactions is much lower than in normal transactions. This suggests we should filter out the transactions and look at them on the right scale. For this, let's use the `dplyr` and filter out the transactions above 300 and look at smaller transactions:

```
df$Class <- as.factor(df$Class)
df %>%filter(Amount<300) %>%ggplot(aes(Class,Amount))+geom_violin()
```

How does the distribution look by class? The following plot tells us something:

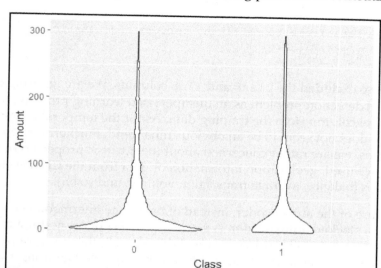

First insight on the data: The amount involved in fraudulent transactions seems more likely to be around 100 than in non-fraudulent transactions.

Aha! So we get our first insight on the data! Fraudulent transactions, although much smaller, are anomalously centered around 100. This might be part of the fraudster's strategy, instead of having large amounts at regular times, they hide small amounts more or less uniformly in time.

Sure, this was fun to find out, but it is definitely not a scalable approach and requires domain knowledge and intuition. It is time to try something more sophisticated.

The autoencoder approach – Keras

OK, time to get into Keras. We should leave apart a small fraction of the data to use as a validation or test set, and develop the model on the remaining. There is no golden standard as to how this should be done. For this example, we will use a 10% test set and a 90% training set:

```
# Remove the time and class column
idxs <- sample(nrow(df), size=0.1*nrow(df))
train <- df[-idxs,]
test <- df[idxs,]
y_train <- train$Class
```

```
y_test <- test$Class
X_train <- train %>% select(-one_of(c("Time","Class")))
X_test <- test %>% select(-one_of(c("Time","Class")))
# Coerce the data frame to matrix to perform the training
X_train <- as.matrix(X_train)
X_test <- as.matrix(X_test)
```

Notice that we also excluded the `Class` and `Time` columns. We are ignoring the label and treating our fraud detection problem as an unsupervised learning problem, hence we need to remove the label column from the training data. As for the temporal information, as we saw before, there does not seem to be an obvious time trend. Furthermore, in real-life fraud detection scenarios, we are rather concerned about the intrinsic properties of the fraudster, for instance, device used, geolocation information or data from the CRM system, as well as account properties (balance, average transaction volume, and so on).

For the architecture of the autoencoder, instead of using one intermediate layer as before, we will now use a **stacked autoencoder**. A stacked autoencoder is nothing more than several layers of encoders, followed by layers of decoders. In this case, we will use a network with outer encoder-decoder layers of 14 fully connected neurons, two inner layers of 7 neurons and yet another inner layer of 7 neurons. You can experiment with different architectures and compare results with ours, there is no universally correct architecture for autoencoders, it relies merely on experience and on diagnosing your model via validation plots and other metrics.

Our input (and output) dimension is `29` in each case. The code to construct the autoencoder is:

```
library(keras)
input_dim <- 29
outer_layer_dim <- 14
inner_layer_dim <- 7
input_layer <- layer_input(shape=c(input_dim))
encoder <- layer_dense(units=outer_layer_dim,
activation='relu')(input_layer)
encoder <- layer_dense(units=inner_layer_dim, activation='relu')(encoder)
decoder <- layer_dense(units=inner_layer_dim)(encoder)
decoder <- layer_dense(units=outer_layer_dim)(decoder)
decoder <- layer_dense(units=input_dim)(decoder)
autoencoder <- keras_model(inputs=input_layer, outputs = decoder)
```

We can look at our work to check everything is correct:

```
autoencoder
 Model
```

Layer (type)	Output Shape	Param #
input_5 (InputLayer)	(None, 29)	0
dense_17 (Dense)	(None, 14)	420
dense_18 (Dense)	(None, 7)	105
dense_22 (Dense)	(None, 7)	56
dense_23 (Dense)	(None, 7)	56
dense_24 (Dense)	(None, 14)	112
dense_25 (Dense)	(None, 29)	435

```
Total params: 1,184
Trainable params: 1,184
Non-trainable params: 0
```

We are now ready to begin our training. We should first compile the model and then fit it:

```
autoencoder %>% compile(optimizer='adam',
                        loss='mean_squared_error',
                        metrics=c('accuracy'))

history <- autoencoder %>% fit(
 X_train,X_train,
 epochs = 10, batch_size = 32,
 validation_split=0.2
 )

plot(history)
```

Our results are shown as follows. You can see that there is an increase in accuracy as the number of epochs increases:

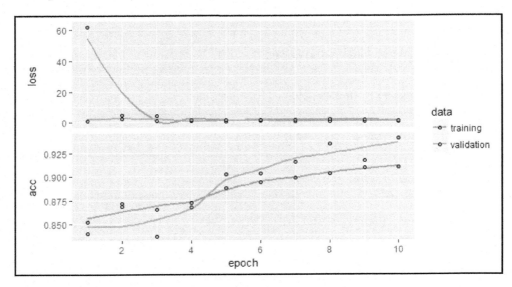

Diagnostic plots for our 14-7-7-7-14 architecture.

Once we have the autoencoder ready, we use it to reconstruct the test set:

```
# Reconstruct on the test set
preds <- autoencoder %>% predict(X_test)
preds <- as.data.frame(preds)
```

We will look for anomalously large reconstruction errors, as before, to be labelled as unusual. For instance, we can look at those points whose reconstruction error is larger than 30 and declare them as unusual:

```
y_preds <- ifelse(rowSums((preds-X_test)**2)/30<1,rowSums((preds-
X_test)**2)/30,1)
```

Again, this threshold is not set in stone, and using your test set in your particular application you can fine-tune it and find the most suitable threshold for your problem.

Finally, let's generate the ROC curve to see if our model is performing correctly using:

```
library(ROCR)
pred <- prediction(y_preds, y_test)
perf <- performance(pred, measure = "tpr", x.measure = "fpr")
plot(perf, col=rainbow(10))
```

We see that the results are satisfactory. Our curve looks quite straight, and the reason for that is that the output of our model is just binary, as well as our original labels. When your model inputs class probabilities, or a proxy for it, then the curve would be smoother:

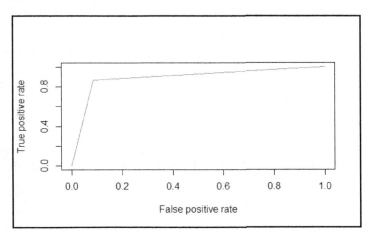

ROC curve: It looks quite straight since the outputs of the model are not class probabilities, but binary.

Fraud detection with H2O

Let's try a slightly different tool, that might help us in real-life deployments. It is often useful to try different tools in the ever-growing data science landscape, if only for sanity0-check purposes.

H2O is an open source software for doing big data analytics. The young start-up (founded in 2016) counts with top researchers in mathematical optimization and statistical learning theory on their advisory board. It runs in standard environments (Linux/Mac/Windows) as well as big data systems and cloud computing environments.

You can run H2O in R, but you need to install the package first:

```
install.packages("h2o")
```

Once this is done, you can load the library:

```
library(h2o)
```

You will then see a welcome message, among some warnings (objects that are masked from other packages):

```
Your next step is to start H2O:
 > h2o.init()
For H2O package documentation, ask for help:
 > ??h2o
After starting H2O, you can use the Web UI at http://localhost:54321
 For more information visit http://docs.h2o.ai
```

So let's do that, and then we will be ready for work:

```
h2o.init()
```

Now we need to read our data into H2O. As the computations work somehow differently, we can not use the vanilla dataframe structure from R, so we either read the file as usual and then coerce it:

```
df <- read.csv("./data/creditcard.csv", stringsAsFactors = F)
 df <- as.h2o(df)
```

Or we read it with the `h2o.uploadFile` function:

```
df2 <- h2o.uploadFile("./data/creditcard.csv")
```

Either way, the resulting structure type is no longer a dataframe, but an environment.

Let's leave aside one portion of the data for training and one for testing, as usual. In `h2o`, we can use the `h2o.splitFrame` function:

```
splits <- h2o.splitFrame(df, ratios=c(0.8), seed=1)
 train <- splits[[1]]
 test <- splits[[2]]
```

Now let's identify between features and label, which will be useful in a minute:

```
label <- "Class"
 features <- setdiff(colnames(train), label)
```

We are ready to start the training of our autoencoder:

```
autoencoder <- h2o.deeplearning(x=features,
 training_frame = train,
 autoencoder = TRUE,
 seed = 1,
 hidden=c(10,2,10),
 epochs = 10,
 activation = "Tanh")
```

Some comments are in order. The autoencoder parameter is set to true, as you would expect. We will use a slightly different architecture this time, just for illustration purposes. You can see in the `hidden` parameter, the structure of the layers. We will also use a different activation function. In practice, it is sometimes useful to use bounded activation functions, such as tanh instead of ReLu, which can be numerically unstable.

We can generate the reconstructions in a similar way as we did with `keras`:

```
# Use the predict function as before
preds <- h2o.predict(autoencoder, test)
```

We get something like this:

```
> head(preds)
  reconstr_Time reconstr_V1 reconstr_V2 reconstr_V3 reconstr_V4 reconstr_V5
reconstr_V6 reconstr_V7
1 380.1466 -0.3041237 0.2373746 1.617792 0.1876353 -0.7355559 0.3570959
-0.1331038
2 1446.0211 -0.2568674 0.2218221 1.581772 0.2254702 -0.6452812 0.4204379
-0.1337738
3 1912.0357 -0.2589679 0.2212748 1.578886 0.2171786 -0.6604871 0.4070894
-0.1352975
4 1134.1723 -0.3319681 0.2431342 1.626862 0.1473913 -0.8192215 0.2911475
-0.1369512
5 1123.6757 -0.3194054 0.2397288 1.619868 0.1612631 -0.7887480 0.3140728
-0.1362253
6 1004.4545 -0.3589335 0.2508191 1.643208 0.1196120 -0.8811920 0.2451117
-0.1380364
```

And from here on, we can proceed as before. However, `h2o` has a built-in function, `h2o.anomaly`, that simplifies part of our work.

Another simplification we can do is instead of importing `ggplot2` and `dplyr` separately, we can import the `tidyverse` package, that brings these (and other) packages useful for data manipulation into our environment:

We call this function and do a bit of formatting to make the row names a column itself, as well as adding the label for the real class:

```
library(tidyverse)
anomaly <- h2o.anomaly(autoencoder, test) %>%
as.data.frame() %>%
tibble::rownames_to_column() %>%
mutate(Class = as.vector(test[, 31]))
```

Let's calculate the average mean square error:

```
# Type coercion useful for plotting later
anomaly$Class <- as.factor(anomaly$Class)
mean_mse <- anomaly %>%
  group_by(Class) %>%
  summarise(mean = mean(Reconstruction.MSE))
```

And finally, visualize our test data as per the reconstruction error:

```
anomaly$Class <- as.factor(anomaly$Class)
mean_mse <- anomaly %>%
    group_by(Class) %>%
    summarise(mean = mean(Reconstruction.MSE))
```

We see that the autoencoder does a not too terrible job. A good proportion of the fraud cases have a relatively high reconstruction error, although it is far from perfect. How could you improve it?:

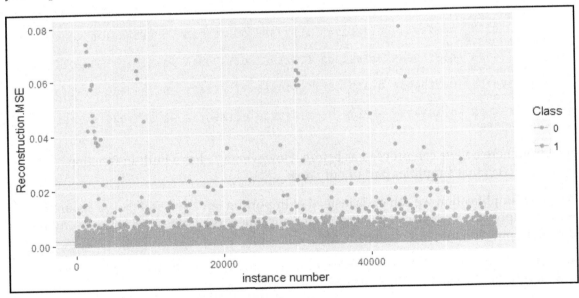

Results from our architecture using H2O, we see that the autoencoder does a good job flagging the fraud cases, but it could still be improved.

Exercises

- We used a mixture of fraud and non-fraud cases in our credit card fraud example. In this case, we are lucky enough to have the correct label for each case. So perhaps in this case, it makes more sense to do the reconstruction of the normal transactions only. Would the detection rate improve if we only used non-fraud cases? Run the same experiment but use only the non-fraud cases for the training set.
- Using the Credit Card dataset, use the reconstructions from the autoencoder as inputs for a classification model, pretty much in the same way you would use PCA. Does this improve the accuracy of the classification? Note that you can do this in this particular dataset, because you have information about the class of the transaction (fraud/non-fraud) which might not be available in other data.

Variational Autoencoders

Variational Autoencoders (**VAE**) are a more recent take on the autoencoding problem. Unlike autoencoders, which learn a compressed representation of the data, Variational Autoencoders learn the random process that generates such data, instead of learning an essentially arbitrary function as we previously did with our neural networks.

VAEs have also an encoder and decoder part. The encoder learns the mean and standard deviation of a normal distribution that is assumed to have generated the data. The mean and standard deviation are called **latent variables** because they are not observed explicitly, rather inferred from the data.

The decoder part of VAEs maps back these latent space points into the data. As before, we need a loss function to measure the difference between the original inputs and their reconstruction. Sometimes an extra term is added, called the **Kullback-Leibler divergence,** or simply KL divergence. The KL divergence computes, roughly, how much a probability distribution differs from another. Adding the KL divergence, forces the posterior distribution to be similar to the prior. This, in turn, helps to both learn better representations of the data and to reduce overfitting.

Unlike autoencoders, VAEs have a solid probabilistic foundation, so the score you get is indeed the probability of an observation being an outlier. In autoencoders, the score we get has no such interpretation, therefore the choice of the cutoff or threshold value is entirely reliant on the input of a human expert, and is strictly data specific.

Image reconstruction using VAEs

Our first example will use the MNIST data to illustrate the use of Variational Autoencoders.

The development strategy is as follows:

- First, an encoder network turns the input samples x, into two parameters in a latent space, which will be denoted z_mean and z_log_sigma
- Then, we randomly sample similar points z from the latent normal distribution which we assumed is used to generate the data, as $z \sim z\_mean + exp(z\_log\_sigma)*epsilon$ where epsilon is a random normal tensor
- Once this is done, a decoder network maps these latent space points z back to the original input data

We begin as usual, getting and preprocessing the data:

```
library(keras)
# Switch to the 1-based indexing from R
options(tensorflow.one_based_extract = FALSE)
K <- keras::backend()
mnist <- dataset_mnist()
X_train <- mnist$train$x
y_train <- mnist$train$y
X_test <- mnist$test$x
y_test <- mnist$test$y
# reshape
dim(X_train) <- c(nrow(X_train), 784)
dim(X_test) <- c(nrow(X_test), 784)
# rescale
X_train <- X_train / 255
X_test <- X_test / 255
```

Note the additional line:

```
K <- keras::backend()
```

This gets us a reference to the tensor backend where Keras will perform the tensor operations.

Now we turn to the VAE. It will consist of a latent dimension of size 2 and a hidden layer of 256 neurons:

```
orig_dim <- 784
latent_dim <- 2
inner_dim <- 256
X <- layer_input(shape = c(original_dim))
hidden_state <- layer_dense(X, intermediate_dim, activation = "relu")
z_mean <- layer_dense(hidden_state, latent_dim)
z_log_sigma <- layer_dense(hidden_state, latent_dim)
```

Next, with the help of our Keras backend, we define the sampling function that will generate the data from the latent variables:

```
sample_z<- function(params){
  z_mean <- params[,0:1]
  z_log_sigma <- params[,2:3]
  epsilon <- K$random_normal(
  shape = c(K$shape(z_mean)[[1]]),
  mean=0.,
  stddev=1
  )
  z_mean + K$exp(z_log_sigma/2)*epsilon
}
```

We now define the sampled points:

```
z <- layer_concatenate(list(z_mean, z_log_sigma)) %>%
  layer_lambda(sample_z)
```

Time to define the decoder. We create separate instances of these layers to be able to reuse them later:

```
decoder_hidden_state <- layer_dense(units = intermediate_dim, activation =
"relu")
decoder_mean <- layer_dense(units = original_dim, activation = "sigmoid")
hidden_state_decoded <- decoder_hidden_state(z)
X_decoded_mean <- decoder_mean(hidden_state_decoded)
```

We are ready! Our VAE is specified by the following encoder and decoder components:

```
# end-to-end autoencoder
variational_autoencoder <- keras_model(X, X_decoded_mean)

encoder <- keras_model(X, z_mean)
decoder_input <- layer_input(shape = latent_dim)
```

```
decoded_hidden_state_2 <- decoder_hidden_state(decoder_input)
decoded_X_mean_2 <- decoder_mean(decoded_hidden_state_2)
generator <- keras_model(decoder_input, decoded_X_mean_2)
```

It remains to specify the custom loss function, since we are adding the KL-divergence penalization:

```
loss_function <- function(X, decoded_X_mean){
  cross_entropy_loss <- loss_binary_crossentropy(X, decoded_X_mean)
  kl_loss <- -0.5*K$mean(1 + z_log_sigma - K$square(z_mean) -
K$exp(z_log_sigma), axis = -1L)
  cross_entropy_loss + kl_loss
}
```

We compile and run our algorithm, as usual:

```
variational_autoencoder %>% compile(optimizer = "rmsprop", loss =
loss_function)
history <- variational_autoencoder %>% fit(
  X_train, X_train,
  shuffle = TRUE,
  epochs = 10,
  batch_size = 256,
  validation_data = list(X_test, X_test)
)
plot(history)
```

After the training is done, we can see the performance (or, follow it in real time using the **Viewer** in RStudio):

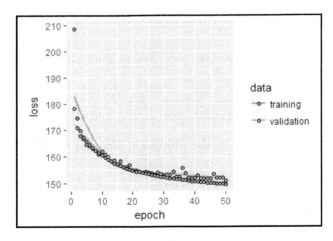

Performance of our for reconstruction in the MNIST data.

We can examine the performance of our algorithm with the following snippet:

```
library(ggplot2)
preds <- variational_autoencoder %>% predict(X_test)
error <- rowSums((preds-X_test)**2)
eval <- data.frame(error=error, class=as.factor(y_test))
eval %>%
 group_by(class) %>%
 summarise(avg_error=mean(error)) %>%
 ggplot(aes(x=class,fill=class,y=avg_error))+geom_col()
```

The results are shown here:

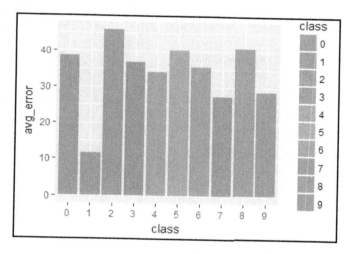

The reconstruction error looks rather discouraging, because we were clearly better off with autoencoders. How could we improve this? One way is to improve the dimension of the latent space. In our current setup, our latent space is only two dimensional. However, note that there is not much lost in terms of quality:

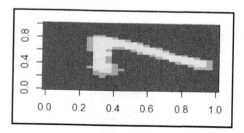

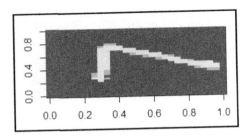

Reconstructed image by our VAE on the left, and the original image on the right (on screen).

Moreover, we now have a generative process! That means that we can create our digits ourselves. Let's loop over the latent space and use the probability distribution to generate our own digits:

```r
# Reshape original and reconstructed
dim(X_test) <- c(nrow(X_test),28,28)
dim(preds) <- c(nrow(preds),28,28)
image(255*preds[1,,], col=gray.colors(3))
y_test[1]
image(255*X_test[1,,], col=gray.colors(3))

grid_x <- seq(-4, 4, length.out = 3)
grid_y <- seq(-4, 4, length.out = 3)

rows <- NULL
for(i in 1:length(grid_x)){
  column <- NULL
  for(j in 1:length(grid_y)){
    z_sample <- matrix(c(grid_x[i], grid_y[j]), ncol = 2)
    column <- rbind(column, predict(generator, z_sample) %>% matrix(ncol =
28) )
  }
  rows <- cbind(rows, column)
}
rows %>% as.raster() %>% plot()
```

Let's look at a few digits generated by our VAE:

Digits generated by the VAE.

Outlier detection in MNIST

Let's look again at the outlier detection problem in MNIST. As before, let's say that the digit 0 is our outlier this time, and we would like to be able to detect it.

We go as before, reading and preprocessing the data:

```
library(keras)
# Switch to the 1-based indexing from R
options(tensorflow.one_based_extract = FALSE)
K <- keras::backend()
mnist <- dataset_mnist()
X_train <- mnist$train$x
y_train <- mnist$train$y
X_test <- mnist$test$x
y_test <- mnist$test$y
## Exclude "0" from the training set. "0" will be the outlier
outlier_idxs <- which(y_train!=0, arr.ind = T)
X_train <- X_train[outlier_idxs,,]
y_test <- sapply(y_test, function(x){ ifelse(x==0,"outlier","normal")})
# reshape
dim(X_train) <- c(nrow(X_train), 784)
dim(X_test) <- c(nrow(X_test), 784)
# rescale
X_train <- X_train / 255
X_test <- X_test / 255
```

Then we define our encoder structure. Note that we will use a different structure of 128 dimensional latent space and 256 neurons in the intermediate layer:

```
original_dim <- 784
latent_dim <- 2
intermediate_dim <- 256
X <- layer_input(shape = c(original_dim))
hidden_state <- layer_dense(X, intermediate_dim, activation = "relu")
z_mean <- layer_dense(hidden_state, latent_dim)
z_log_sigma <- layer_dense(hidden_state, latent_dim)
```

And rewrite our `sample_z` function to make it easier to customize:

```
sample_z<- function(params){
  z_mean <- params[,0:1]
  z_log_sigma <- params[,2:3]
  epsilon <- K$random_normal(
    shape = c(K$shape(z_mean)[[1]]),
    mean=0.,
    stddev=1
```

```
  )
  z_mean + K$exp(z_log_sigma/2)*epsilon
}
```

Then we go for the decoder part:

```
z <- layer_concatenate(list(z_mean, z_log_sigma)) %>%
  layer_lambda(sample_z)
decoder_hidden_state <- layer_dense(units = intermediate_dim, activation =
"relu")
decoder_mean <- layer_dense(units = original_dim, activation = "sigmoid")
hidden_state_decoded <- decoder_hidden_state(z)
X_decoded_mean <- decoder_mean(hidden_state_decoded)
```

And finally, the full autoencoder:

```
variational_autoencoder <- keras_model(X, decoded_X_mean)
encoder <- keras_model(X, z_mean)
decoder_input <- layer_input(shape = latent_dim)
decoded_hidden_state_2 <- decoder_hidden_state(decoder_input)
decoded_X_mean_2 <- decoder_mean(decoded_hidden_state_2)
generator <- keras_model(decoder_input, decoded_X_mean_2)
```

We define loss function with:

```
loss_function <- function(X, decoded_X_mean){
  cross_entropy_loss <- loss_binary_crossentropy(X, decoded_X_mean)
  kl_loss <- -0.5*K$mean(1 + z_log_sigma - K$square(z_mean) -
K$exp(z_log_sigma), axis = -1L)
  cross_entropy_loss + kl_loss
}
```

We use the same function as before and train the model:

```
variational_autoencoder %>% compile(optimizer = "rmsprop", loss =
loss_function)
history <- variational_autoencoder %>% fit(
  X_train, X_train,
  shuffle = TRUE,
  epochs = 10,
  batch_size = 256,
  validation_data = list(X_test, X_test)
)
plot(history)
```

Once the training is done, we look at the performance:

```
preds <- variational_autoencoder %>% predict(X_test)
error <- rowSums((preds-X_test)**2)
eval <- data.frame(error=error, class=as.factor(y_test))
library(dplyr)
library(ggplot2)
eval %>%
  ggplot(aes(x=class,fill=class,y=error))+geom_boxplot()
```

Let's look at the reconstruction error per class:

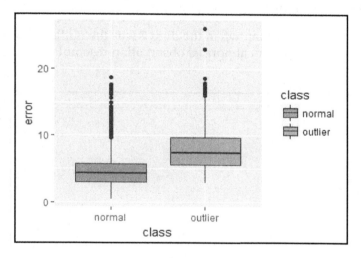

Reconstruction error using the VAE.

The plot suggests you set a reconstruction error for the threshold as 5:

```
threshold <- 5
y_preds <- sapply(error,
function(x){ifelse(x>threshold,"outlier","normal")})
```

And we now look at the confusion matrix:

```
table(y_preds,y_test)
         y_test
y_preds normal outlier
  outlier 9020     980
```

Which suggests that we are on the right track! But before celebrating, we should look at the other classification metrics, the ROC curve and the area under this curve (AUC):

```
library(ROCR)
pred <- prediction(error, y_test)
perf <- performance(pred, measure = "tpr", x.measure = "fpr")
auc <- unlist(performance(pred, measure = "auc")@y.values)
auc
plot(perf, col=rainbow(10))
```

We get an AUC of 0.8473375 and a reasonable ROC plot shown as follows, which tells us that our VAE did a good job distinguishing the outlier 0.

Note that this was much better than when the digit 7 was the outlier. This tells us that we need to put in extra effort when an abnormal observation resembles the usual observations too much:

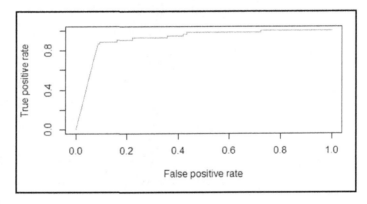

ROC curve for our variational autoencoder.

Text fraud detection

Fraud has become an issue beyond the traditional transaction fraud. Many websites, for instance, rely on user reviews about services, such as restaurants, hotels or tourist attractions, that are monetized in different ways. If the users lose trust in those reviews, for example, by a business owner deliberately messing with the good reviews for his or her own business, then the website will find it hard to regain that trust and to remain profitable. Hence, it is important to detect such potential issues.

How can autoencoders help us with this? As before, the idea is to learn the representation of a *normal* review on a website, and then find those that do not fit the *normal* review. The issue with text data is that there is some processing to be done before. We will illustrate this with an example, which will also serve as a motivation for the different ways of modelling text that will be discussed in the next chapters.

From unstructured text data to a matrix

An issue with text data is that words and sentences are messy, and algorithms for data mining usually do not work out of the box, as they are designed to operate on abstractions of the data, usually in matrix form. So we need to find a way to represent our messy text data as a matrix.

One of the most commonly used matrix representations in practice is the *bag of words* model. This is a very simple and intuitive way of extracting information from text. There are some caveats to it, which will be discussed later.

A bag of words representation of a text consists of:

- A vocabulary of known words
- A numerical measure associated to the presence of such words

For example, suppose we have a *corpus* (a collection of documents) consisting of three sentences:

- `"My sentence"`
- `"Your sentence"`
- `"My sentence, your sentence, our sentences"`

The vocabulary (ignoring the comma) is the collection (`"My"`, `"sentence"`, `"sentences"`, `"Your"`, `"your"`, `"our"`). As for the numerical measure, a natural option would be the count function. So the matrix representation would be:

My	Your	sentence	sentences	your	our
1	0	1	0	0	0
0	1	1	0	0	0
1	0	2	1	1	1

This is now something we can operate with. Note that a few comments are in order. We ignored the comma, which does not seem like a big deal, but it is, and we will come back to it. Second, we are including "Your" and "your" as different words, which is probably not desirable. Note that also "sentence" and "sentences" are similar from the information point of view. If we want to infer the content of a document, it might suffice to keep just one of them.

To deal with the capitalization issue, we can simply convert all the words to lower case first, before passing to the matrix form. Dealing with plurals or other derived words from a *root* word is done through different algorithms, called **stemmers**. The most common choice is Porter's stemming algorithm. Sometimes it is not a good idea to do stemming, it might depend on the language and the context of your problem.

Depending on the context, sometimes common words such as pronouns are better omitted. There are lists of such words, called **stop words** readily available on the internet. So before creating the matrix representation, you filter those words, which also reduces the dimension of the problem.

A problem with scoring word frequency is that we will have highly frequent words dominating the matrix representation, but this domination might be useless from the information point of view. Instead, what is done often is to use alternative representations such as TF–IDF, which stands for text document-inverse document frequency. There are different ways to calculate it, roughly equivalent, if w is a word, D is the set of documents and d is a document there (in the preceding example, one of the sentences), then:

$$tfidf(w, d, D) = \frac{\text{frequency of w in d}}{\text{number of documents in D that have w in them}}$$

You can play around with these, for example, instead of frequency of word in the numerator, you can use the characteristic function (0 if the word is not there, 1 if it is), or the logarithm of that. Similarly, you can consider different possibilities for the denominator.

The issue with removing the punctuation is a bit more subtle, and it has to do with the main disadvantage of the bag of words approach, meaning is completely lost. Even without considering punctuation, sentences like `Alice loves pizza` and `Pizza loves Alice` would be represented identically, but they have different meanings. With punctuation, we can get completely opposite meanings, the sentences `Pardon, impossible execution` and `Pardon impossible, execution` mean opposite things.

Context is also lost, and relations within words might be lost. For instance, the documents I was in Paris and I saw the Eiffel tower are clearly related, but they would appear as orthogonal documents in a bag of words representation. We will address some of these issues in later chapters.

From text to matrix representation — the Enron dataset

The Enron email dataset contains approximately 500,000 emails generated by employees of the Enron Corporation. It was obtained by the Federal Energy Regulatory Commission of the United States during its investigation of Enron's collapse. The Enron corporation was an American energy company based in Houston, Texas, that was involved in an accountant fraud scandal that eventually led to its bankruptcy. We will use a subset as an example, but you can access the full dataset (500,000 emails) from Kaggle, (https://www.kaggle.com/wcukierski/enron-email-dataset) or from the Computer Science school in Carnegie Mellon University (https://www.cs.cmu.edu/~./enron/).

For text mining, we will use the packages, tm (https://cran.r-project.org/web/packages/tm/index.html) and SnowballC (https://cran.r-project.org/web/packages/SnowballC/index.html). Be sure to install them before:

```
install.packages("tm")
install.packages("SnowballC")
```

We start by loading the dataframe in our workspace. We will omit some of the preprocessing stems and assume that your dataframe has two columns, email and responsive. We hand-label the responsive column for our small sample, if not available from the original data (not all versions have it). Responsive means, in legal terms, whether the email is relevant to the fraud investigation:

```
df <- read.csv("./data/enron.csv")
names(df)
[1] "email"       "responsive"
```

We load the tm library and create a corpus object from the email column:

```
library(tm)
corpus <- Corpus(VectorSource(df$email))
```

We can access each email with the inspect command, as follows:

```
inspect(corpus[[1]])
```

A series of transformations are applied to our data before modeling: converting to lower case, remove punctuation, stop words and stemming:

```
corpus <- tm_map(corpus,tolower)
corpus <- tm_map(corpus, removePunctuation)
corpus <- tm_map(corpus, removeWords, stopwords("english"))
corpus <- tm_map(corpus, stemDocument)
```

Once this is done, we are ready to obtain a matrix representation of the documents, as follows:

```
dtm <- DocumentTermMatrix(corpus)
dtm <-   removeSparseTerms(dtm, 0.97)
X <- as.data.frame(as.matrix(dtm))
X$responsive <- df$responsive
```

We create the train/test split. For this, we can use the library `caTools`:

```
# Train, test, split
library(caTools)
set.seed(42)
spl <- sample.split(X$responsive, 0.7)
train <- subset(X, spl == TRUE)
test <- subset(X, spl == FALSE)
train <- subset(train, responsive==0)
```

Autoencoder on the matrix representation

Once we put the text in matrix form, we can continue the training of the autoencoder, as in the previous sections.

Note that our autoencoder will have only non-responsive emails on the training part. This turns out to be quite helpful in this dataset, which has only a few hundred samples.

Once this is done, we create our training and testing sets, splitting in X and y components as before:

```
X_train <- subset(train,select=-responsive)
y_train <- train$responsive
X_test <- subset(test,select=-responsive)
y_test <- test$responsive
```

Now, we are ready to define our autoencoder. We will use only an inner layer with size 32:

```
library(keras)
input_dim <- ncol(X_train)
inner_layer_dim <- 32
input_layer <- layer_input(shape=c(input_dim))
encoder <- layer_dense(units=inner_layer_dim,
activation='relu')(input_layer)
decoder <- layer_dense(units=input_dim)(encoder)
autoencoder <- keras_model(inputs=input_layer, outputs = decoder)
autoencoder %>% compile(optimizer='adam',
                        loss='mean_squared_error',
                        metrics=c('accuracy'))
```

Then, for the training:

```
X_train <- as.matrix(X_train)
X_test <- as.matrix(X_test)
history <- autoencoder %>% fit(
 X_train,X_train,
 epochs = 100, batch_size = 32,
 validation_data = list(X_test, X_test)
)
plot(history)
```

We look at the reconstruction on the test set and look at the distribution of errors across both classes:

```
# Reconstruct on the test set
preds <- autoencoder %>% predict(X_test)
error <- rowSums((preds-X_test)**2)
library(tidyverse)
eval %>%
 filter(error < 1000) %>%
 ggplot(aes(x=error,color=class))+geom_density()
```

As usual, let's take a look at the distribution of error per class, this time with a density plot:

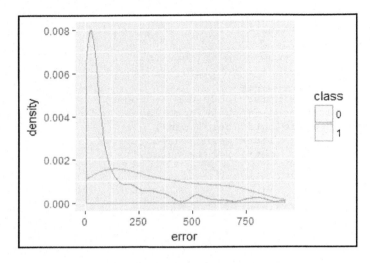

Distribution of the reconstruction error per class.

Note that we filtered on the reconstruction error, As before, this helps us look at the scale on where the majority of the observations are. Our goal is to set a threshold for the reconstruction error, to flag as outlier (which in this context means that the email is not an ordinary email communication). Visually, it seems that 100 is a reasonable threshold, although we will get a high number of false positives:

```
threshold <- 100
y_preds <- sapply(error,
function(x){ifelse(x>threshold,"outlier","normal")})
# Confusion matrix
table(y_preds,y_test)
         y_test
y_preds   0 1
 normal  142 7
 outlier 73 35
```

We do a reasonably good job catching the suspicious emails, at the cost of 73 false positives. There is always a trade off between catching a high number of false positives and ignoring true positives. The model could be improved by adding more data, we used only around 800 emails from 500,000 available, so clearly there is room for improvement. The model works reasonably well, nonetheless, as confirmed by the AUC value of 0.79 and the ROC plot:

```
library(ROCR)
pred <- prediction(error, y_test)
perf <- performance(pred, measure = "tpr", x.measure = "fpr")
auc <- unlist(performance(pred, measure = "auc")@y.values)
plot(perf, col=rainbow(10))
auc
[1] 0.7951274
plot(perf, col=rainbow(10))
```

We see the ROC curve for the Enron dataset, as follows. This allows us to diagnose our model for binary classifiers in general, not only in this case:

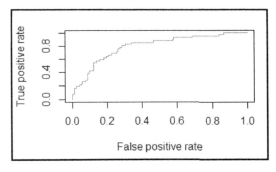

ROC curve for the Enron dataset.

Exercises

- Use the original Enron dataset to create an autoencoder that would identify suspicious from non-suspicious emails.
- Instead of an autoencoder, you can try with Variational Autoencoders. Compare the performance of both approaches.

Summary

In this chapter, we learned that autoencoders are a technique used mainly in image reconstruction and denoising, to obtain compressed and summarized representations of the data. We saw that they are also used sometimes for fraud detection tasks. The outlier identification comes from measuring the reconstruction error, observing the distribution of the reconstruction error, we can set up thresholds for identifying the outliers and learn the probabilistic process that generates the data. Hence, Variational Autoencoders are also able to generate new data.

4
Text Generation Using Recurrent Neural Networks

In this chapter, we will describe some of the most exciting techniques in modern (at the time of writing—late 2017) machine learning, recurrent neural networks. They are, however, not new; they have been around since the 1980s, but they have become popular due to the numerous records in language-related tasks in recent years.

Why do we need a different type of architecture for text? Consider the following example:

"I live in Prague since 2015"

and

"Since 2015 I live in Prague"

If we would like to teach a traditional feed-forward network such as a perceptron or a multi-layer perceptron to identify the date I moved to Prague, then this network would have to learn separate parameters for each input feature, which in particular implies that it would have to learn grammar to answer this simple question! This is undesirable in many applications. Similar issues motivated machine learning researchers and statisticians in the 1980s to introduce the idea of sharing parameters across different parts of the model. This idea is the secret sauce of recurrent neural networks, our next deep learning architecture.

By design, recurrent neural networks are well-suited for processing sequential data. In general, machine learning applied to sequential data can be roughly divided into four main areas:

- Sequence prediction: Given $[x_{t-2}, x_{t-1}, x_t]$, predict the next element of the sequence, x_{t+1}
- Sequence classification: Given $[x_{t-2}, x_{t-1}, x_t]$, predict a category or label for it
- Sequence generation: Given $[x_{t-2}, x_{t-1}, x_t]$, generate a new element of the sequence, x_{t+1}
- Sequence to sequence prediction: Given $[x_{t-2}, x_{t-1}, x_t]$, generate an equivalent sequence, $[y_{t-1}, y_t, y_{t+1}]$

Applications of sequence prediction include weather forecasting and stock market prediction. For classification, we can think, for example, of sentiment analysis and document classification. Automatic image captioning or text generation are part of the sequence generation family of problems, whereas machine translation might be the most familiar example of sequence to sequence prediction we see in our everyday lives.

Our focus for this chapter is on applications of recurrent neural networks for text generation. Since, as we saw previously, text generation is part of a much larger set of problems, many of our algorithms are portable to other contexts.

Training deep learning models is often time-consuming, and recurrent neural networks are not the exception. Our focus is on the ideas over the data, which we will illustrate with smaller datasets than those that you might encounter later on in the wild. This is for the purpose of clarity: We want to make it easier for you to get started on any standard laptop. Once you grasp the basics, you can spin off your own cluster in your favorite cloud provider.

What is so exciting about recurrent neural networks?

Coming from a mathematics background, in my rather hectic career I have seen many different trends, particularly during the last few years, which all sound very similar to me: *"you have a problem? wavelets can save you!"*, *"finite elements are the solution to everything"*, and similar over-enthusiastic claims.

Of course, each tool has its time and place and, more importantly, an application domain where it excels. I find recurrent neural networks quite interesting for the many features they can achieve:

- Produce consistent markup text (opening and closing tags, recognizing timestamp-like data)
- Write Wikipedia articles with references, and create URLs from non-existing addresses, by learning what a URL should look like
- Create credible-looking scientific papers from LaTeX

All these amazing features are possible without the network having any context information or metadata. In particular, without knowing English, nor what a URL or a bit of LaTeX syntax looks like.

These and even more interesting capabilities of neural networks are superbly described by Andrej Karpathy in *The Unreasonable Effectiveness of Recurrent Neural Networks:* `http://karpathy.github.io/2015/05/21/rnn-effectiveness/`.

 What makes recurrent neural networks exciting? Instead of a constrained fixed-input size to fixed-output size, we can operate over sequences of vectors instead.

A limitation of many machine learning algorithms, including standard feed-forward neural networks, is that they accept a fixed size vector as input and produce a fixed size vector as output. For instance, if we want to classify text, we receive a corpus of documents from which we create a vocabulary to vectorize each document and the output is a vector with class probabilities. Recurrent neural networks instead allow us to take sequences of vectors as input. So, from a one-to-one correspondence between fixed input size and fixed output size, we have a much richer landscape, one-to-one, one-to-many, many-to-one, many-to-many.

Why is that desirable? Let's look at a few examples:

- **One-to-one**: Supervised learning, for instance, text classification
- **One-to-many**: Given an input text, generate a summary (a sequence of words with important information)
- **Many-to-one**: Sentiment analysis in text
- **Many-to-many**: Machine translation

Moreover, as recurrent neural networks maintain an internal state which gets updated according to new information, we can view RNNs as a description of a program. In fact, a paper by Siegelman in 1995 shows that recurrent neural networks are Turing complete, they can simulate arbitrary programs.

But what is a recurrent neural network, really?

How does the network keep track of the previous states? To put it in the context of text generation, think of our training data as a list of character sequences (tokenized words). For each word, from the first character, we will predict the following:

Formally, let's denote a sequence of $t+1$ characters as $x = [x_0, x_1, x_2, \ldots, x_t]$. Let $s_{-1} = 0$.

For $k=0,2,\ldots t$, we construct the following sequence:

$$s_k = \tanh(Ux_k + Ws_{k-1})$$
$$o_k = \text{softmax}(Vs_k)$$

This is summarized in the following diagram, when input x is received, the internal state, s, of the network is modified, and then used to generate an output, o:

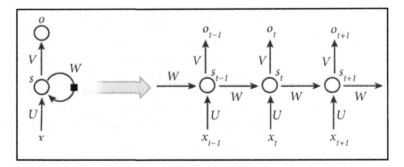

Figure 1: Information flow for an RNN. The representations are equivalent; the unfolded representation hints at how backpropagation could work in this setup.

The hidden state, s, need not be one-dimensional, as you might have imagined. Of course, it should not be too big, otherwise you might experience overfitting. A good way to start is to choose a hidden layer one order of magnitude smaller than the input space, so that if your input vector has lives in a thousand-dimensional space (not uncommon in text problems), then your hidden state should be in the hundreds.

A traditional deep neural network uses different parameters at each layer. In a recurrent neural network, the parameters are shared across all time steps (see preceding *Figure 1*) across all steps. This reflects the fact that the task is the same (in this case, *reading*), just with different inputs. It also helps to reduce the number of parameters we need to learn.

We choose the `tanh` function because it puts the inputs in the range [-1,1]. Later, we will want to use the outputs of the network as probabilities; the output layer is the *softmax* function.

The diagram shown in *Figure 1* fully describes the **forward propagation** of our network, given the weight matrices, we can calculate the output of the network. But how should we train the network to find those weights?

As usual in neural networks, the idea is to use the difference between the predictions of the network and the training labels to adjust the weights in the right direction. For this, we need to specify a loss function. A common choice is the cross-entropy loss function:

$$L(y, o) := -\frac{1}{N} \sum_{n \in N} y_n \log o_n$$

Where N denotes the number of training examples. This function measures a weighted score on the predicted class times the log probability of that class. Note that we get a loss of zero if we have probability of 1 for the correct class, and a positive loss otherwise. This means that the cross entropy punishes us for not being confident. Notice that it also punishes us for being confident and incorrect (why is that?).

To update the weights, we need to compute the derivatives:

$$\frac{\partial L}{\partial U}, \frac{\partial L}{\partial V}, \frac{\partial L}{\partial W}$$

We also need to update the weights in the direction that reduces the error, that is, the opposite direction of the gradient. This sounds no more complicated than vanilla backpropagation in standard neural networks. The situation is a bit more complicated in recurrent neural networks because of the hidden state, which links the current time step with the previous history. To see this, let's say that we want to compute the partial derivative of the loss function with respect to W. We need to calculate:

$$\frac{\partial L}{\partial W} := \frac{\partial L}{\partial o_t} \cdot \frac{\partial o_t}{\partial s_t} \cdot \frac{\partial s_t}{\partial W}$$

Nothing strange here, simply using the chain rule. What's the trick? The catch is in the second and third term in the preceding expression. The internal state at time t depends on the internal state at the previous time. Hence, our computation is actually:

$$\frac{\partial L}{\partial W} = \frac{\partial L}{\partial o_t} \cdot \frac{\partial o_t}{\partial s_t} \cdot \frac{\partial s_t}{\partial s_{t-1}} \cdot \frac{\partial s_{t-1}}{\partial s_{t-2}} \cdots \frac{\partial s_1}{\partial W}$$

You can see how this computation should be done from the preceding diagram, showing the unfolded version of the network. The preceding computation is a different form of the backpropagation algorithm, called **backpropagation through time**.

An important consequence of the preceding is that recurrent neural networks are hard to train. Since the derivative of the `tanh` function is bounded by 1, in the preceding computation, we see a lot of terms multiplying each other between 0 and 1. So the resulting gradient will be small, and it might become numerically zero early on in the training. This is quite bad, because this prevents from learning long-term dependencies. This is because the gradient contributions from *far away* steps become zero because, in line with the chain rule, they are the product of many numbers less than 1. This problem is known as the vanishing gradient problem and was first discovered by Sepp Hochreiter in 1991. It is by no means exclusive of recurrent neural networks. Standard feed-forward neural networks have the same issue when you have many layers (we say they are deep when they have four or more layers), it is just that recurrent neural networks tend to be very deep; as deep as the sentence length, in our case.

There are a few ways to address the vanishing gradient problem, you can use the ReLU function, which in R notation is:

```
ifelse(x>0,x,0)
```

This function has a gradient of 0 or 1, hence it helps us to avoid the vanishing gradient issue. Relevant sections of the parameter space will be explored, even if they correspond to changes in the *far-away* history. Another possibility is to use different mechanisms, such as LSTM networks, proposed by Hochreiter and Schmidhuber in 1997, or GRU networks, by Cho and coauthors in 2014. We will describe these networks briefly in the next section.

Besides the vanishing gradient problem, you can imagine that, depending on the structure of the network and the activation functions you choose, you can have the opposite situation, exploding gradients. This can happen, for instance, if the Jacobian has very small values. This is somehow less serious because you will get a `NaN` error on your code. One way around it is to clip the gradients, this simply means that you should add a condition that filters out values above a certain threshold. Of course, this will depend on your particular application and you might want to take a look at different values in certain cases.

The main complication for implementing different types of neural networks is the computation of the gradients. In simple cases, this can be done by hand, but, as you can see, things quickly get out of control.

Once the gradients are obtained, there are different methods we can use, perhaps the most popular being stochastic gradient descent. Unfortunately, stochastic gradient descent is not *plug and play*. You need to spend some time messing with the step size hyperparameter to get it to work properly. This is quite bad for working with neural networks. Other solutions, such as **Adagrad**, are used in practice. Adagrad is particularly simple to implement, and we will do so later in this chapter. The learning rate is adapted component-wise, and is given by the square root of the sum of squares of the historical, component-wise gradient. Other optimizers include RMSProp and Adam. An advantage, or at least a theoretical guarantee of Adagrad, is that it has a sound theory behind it, rather than being heuristic.

It is possible to optimize a recurrent neural network without relying on gradient methods. For instance, by using genetic or evolutionary algorithms. Evolutionary algorithms are good for finding global minima in some cases, as by avoiding the direction of the gradient, they can find better solutions. A drawback of such algorithms is that they can be quite computing-intensive.

LSTM and GRU networks

As we saw, the recursive structure of RNN and LSTM networks have problems with gradients, either the gradients vanish or explode. One workaround is to introduce forget gates, which will delete some of the old information. This helps to keep track of relevant information without destroying the gradients, and to better preserve important data observed a long time ago.

Both LSTM and GRU share the same design principle with recurrent neural networks, give an input, compute an output, and then a black box updates the internal state. This is crucial in order to understand the bigger picture.

LSTM

For an LSTM, we compute a number of things:

- An input gate, i
- A forget gate, f
- An output gate, o
- A candidate internal state, g

- An internal memory of the unit, c
- A final internal state, s

These are defined by the following recursive equations:

$$i = \sigma(U^i x_t + W^i s_{t-1})$$
$$f = \sigma(U^f x_t + W^f s_{t-1})$$
$$o = \sigma(U^o x_t + W^o s_{t-1})$$
$$g = \tanh(U^g x_t + W^g s_{t-1})$$
$$c_t = c_{t-1} \cdot f + g \cdot i$$
$$s_t = \tanh(c_t) \cdot o$$

Where:

$$\sigma(x) := \frac{1}{1 + e^{-x}}$$

The first three equations describe the input, forget, and output gates. They are called **gates** because they decide which fraction of the newly computed candidate state will be allowed through, and which fraction will be forgotten. Given the new observations, we might want to keep something from the old memories and delete other things, or decide how much of the new information to take into account. This is computed in the memory variable, c. Finally, given this memory update, we keep a fraction of it that will be used by other parts of the network. If the weights in the input gate are all set to 1, the weights in the forget gate are all set to 0 and the weights of the output gate are all set to 1. We almost recover standard recurrent neural networks, except that the activation layer will have an extra `tanh`.

There are many variations of LSTM architectures, building on this basic model. Examples include convolutional, bi-directional, peephole, and LSTM with a forget gate. A great resource is Chris Olah's blog post on the topic: `http://colah.github.io/posts/2015-08-Understanding-LSTMs/`.

GRU

Gated recurrent units (GRUs) share a similar design philosophy to LSTM layers. They consist of:

- A hidden state, h
- An internal state, s

- An update gate, z
- A reset gate, r

The updates are given by the following recurrence relations:

$$z = \sigma(U^z x_t + W^z s_{t-1})$$
$$r = \sigma(U^r x_t + W^r s_{t-1})$$
$$h = \tanh(U^h x_t + W^h(s_{t-1} r))$$
$$s_t = (1 - z) \cdot h + z \cdot s_{t-1}$$

The reset gate tells us how to put together the input with the previous memory. The update gate defines how much of the previous memory we should keep for the next iteration. This helps the network to forget useless things, and create connections with newer evidence. The resulting network has no hidden memory (c) which is independent of the internal state, as in the case with LSTMs. They also have input and forget gates merged into the update gate. One more key difference is that there is no second non-linearity (the second call to `tanh` in LSTMs) when computing the final output.

So, which one to use? The jury is still out on that one. There is no conclusive evidence to use one network over another. GRUs have fewer parameters and may be a bit faster to train. They also might need less data to generalize well (as it is easier to estimate the weights accurately). GRUs are quite new, from 2014, so they have not been very well-explored.

RNNs from scratch in R

The purpose of this section is to show you how you can implement recurrent neural networks from bare bones in R. This is perhaps not the optimal solution for a number of reasons, but it is a great way to get started in deep learning.

There are many *plug and play* frameworks like H2O, MXNet, TensorFlow, or Keras, that have compatibility with R. Our goal is to focus on the understanding of the algorithm rather than a particular API, although we will include an example using Keras. This is for two reasons, at the time of writing, the compatibility with R suffers from growing pains and we encountered many errors and issues with the different packages. On the other hand, even the stable versions of such packages have ever-changing APIs. We will focus on this section in building a very simple recurrent neural network from scratch, using simple tools from R.

We will start from the beginning, with a super-quick introduction to R6 classes in R using the example of the perceptron, and incrementally build from there.

Classes in R with R6

The R language supports object oriented programming, although there is no universal standard for class definition. R has different class systems, S3, S4, R5, and R6. Since R is, in its origins, a statistics playground software, some features from modern general purpose programming languages are not present there. Complex projects are a bit harder to write, as a result, but not impossible, and the situation keeps improving thanks to the community support.

Why the name R6? As per the official R documentation (https://cran.r-project.org/web/packages/R6/vignettes/Introduction.html), R6 is the successor of the package R5, whose development was halted. R6 is an attempt to improve some deficiencies in S3 and S4. It is also the recommended method to implement self-modifying objects, as is the case here. We need to change the weights of the network as the training progresses.

How do we define an R6 class? Let's show you this with an example in the next section.

Perceptron as an R6 class

The perceptron is the simplest neural network. It consists of an input and an output (no hidden layers), and the activation function is just the Heaviside function (step function at the origin), when the bias term is included.

This is the skeleton of the class:

```
library(R6)
Perceptron <- R6Class("Perceptron",
 public = list(
     threshold = NULL,
     dim = NULL,
     n_iter = NULL,
     learning_rate = NULL,
     w = NULL,
 initialize = function(threshold = 0, learning_rate = 0.25, n_iter=100,
dim=2){
     self$n_iter <- n_iter
     self$threshold <- threshold
     self$learning_rate <- learning_rate
 }
 , forward = function(x){
     }
 , backward = function(t,y,x){
     }
```

```
        }
    , train = function(X,t){
        }
    }
    }
    }
    , predict = function(X){
        X <- cbind(-1,X) #add bias
        preds <- c()
        for(i in 1:nrow(X)){
        preds[i] <- self$forward(X[i,])
    }
    return(preds)
    }
    )
)
```

Although R6 supports private methods, we do not really need them at this point; we can live with public methods, which are specified previously. Note that you do need to initialize with NULL all the objects you plan to use; failing to do so will result in errors.

Now we can implement the perceptron, filling in the blanks in the preceding function:

```
library(R6)
Perceptron <- R6Class("Perceptron",
 public = list(
     threshold = NULL,
     dim = NULL,
     n_iter = NULL,
     learning_rate = NULL,
     w = NULL,
     initialize = function(threshold = 0,
                             learning_rate = 0.25,
                             n_iter=100, dim=2)
                       {
                       self$n_iter <- n_iter
                       self$threshold <- threshold
                       self$learning_rate <- learning_rate
                       self$dim <- dim
                       self$w <- matrix(runif(self$dim+1), ncol = self$dim+1)
                       }
    , forward = function(x){
                dot_product <- sum(x*self$w)
                y <- ifelse(dot_product>self$threshold,1,0)
                return(y)
        }
    , backward = function(t,y,x){
```

```
                    for(j in 1:ncol(x)){
                        self$w[j] <- self$w[j]+self$learning_rate*(t-y)*x[j]
                }
        }
    , train = function(X,t){
                    X <- cbind(-1,X) #add bias term
                    n_examples <- nrow(X)

                    for(iter in 1:self$n_iter){
                        for(i in 1:nrow(X)){
                            y_i <- self$forward(X[i,])
                            self$backward(t[i],y_i, X[i,])
                            }
                        if(iter %% 20 == 0){
                            cat("Iteration: ", iter)
                            print("Weights: ")
                            print(unlist(self$w))
                            }
                    }
    }
    , predict = function(X){
                    X <- cbind(-1,X) #add bias
                    preds <- c()
                    for(i in 1:nrow(X)){
                        preds[i] <- self$forward(X[i,])
                        }
            return(preds)
        }
    )
    )
```

How can you test that your implementation is correct? Well, your network should be able to predict correctly the labels of the following data (the OR function) after a few iterations:

x1	x2	t
0	0	0
1	0	1
0	1	1
1	1	1

To test your implementation, you need first to create a data frame with this dataset:

```
x1 <- c(0,0,1,1)
x2 <- c(0,1,0,1)
t <- c(0,1,1,1)
X <- data.frame(x1=x1, x2=x2)
```

Now, let's initialize:

```
lr <- LR$new(n_iter=100, dim=ncol(X))
lr
```

Next, we call the `train` method:

```
lr$train(X,t)
lr$w
```

And, finally, `predict`:

```
lr$predict(X)
```

To get an insight into what the perceptron is doing, we will draw the decision boundary, that is, the criteria the algorithm is using for classification.

First, we coerce to a data frame, as we will use the `ggplot2` library:

```
df <- as.data.frame(X)
df$t <- as.factor(t)
```

Then, we get the coefficients:

```
# Get the line
w0 <- as.numeric(lr$w[1])
w1 <- as.numeric(lr$w[2])
w2 <- as.numeric(lr$w[3])
```

And finally, we create the line:

```
x1_vals <- seq(-0.15,1,0.1)
x2_vals <- (w0-w1*x1_vals)/w2
boundary <- data.frame(x1_vals=x1_vals, x2_vals=x2_vals)

#Plot decision boundary
library(ggplot2)
ggplot()+
    geom_point(data=df, aes(x=x1,y=x2, color=t, size=2))+
    geom_line(data=boundary, aes(x=x1_vals, y=x2_vals, size=1))+
    theme_bw()
```

This gives us the following output:

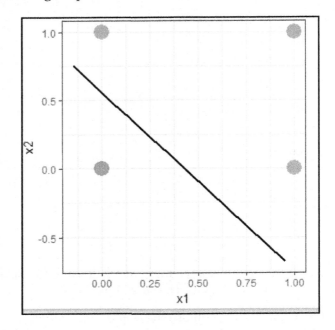

The OR function and the decision boundary

This shows us that the perceptron can separate this dataset in a non-unique way.

The functionality of the perceptron is quite limited, and it is only shown here to illustrate the way to implement classes in R. For instance, the perceptron is unable to separate simple examples as the one shown as follows:

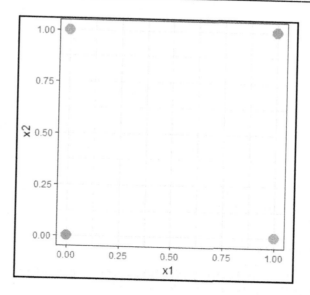

The XOR function

As you can see, there is no way to draw a line that separates both classes, hence showing the limitations of the perceptron.

There are two ways around this. One is to create additional features, like *x1*x2*, which would indeed make the data separable. The other way is to create a more complicated decision mechanism (a non-linear decision boundary). We will, in some sense, show you how to do the second.

Logistic regression

We can, in a very similar way, implement logistic regression as an R6 class. The code is included just for intellectual curiosity, as it is closely related.

There is not a lot of difference between the perceptron and logistic regression. They share a lot in common, the main difference being the activation function (logit instead of the Heaviside step function), which also changes the update rule for the weights. For convenience, we highlight in bold the more relevant differences:

```
library(R6)
logit <- function(x){
  1/(1+exp(-x))
}
LR <- R6Class("LR",
```

```
        public = list(
        dim = NULL,
        n_iter = NULL,
        learning_rate = NULL,
        w = NULL,
        initialize = function(learning_rate = 0.25, n_iter=100, dim=2){
            self$n_iter <- n_iter
            self$learning_rate <- learning_rate
            self$dim <- dim
            self$w <- matrix(runif(self$dim+1), ncol = self$dim+1)
    }
  , forward = function(x){
            dot_product <- sum(x*self$w)
            y <- logit(dot_product)
            return(y)
        }
  , backward = function(t,y,x){
            for(j in 1:ncol(x)){
            self$w[j] <- self$w[j]+self$learning_rate*(t-
y)*x[j]*logit(x[j])*(1-logit(x[j]))
    }

    }
  , train = function(X,t){
            X <- cbind(-1,X) #add bias term
            n_examples <- nrow(X)

  for(iter in 1:self$n_iter){
      for(i in 1:nrow(X)){
      y_i <- self$forward(X[i,])
      self$backward(t[i],y_i, X[i,])
  }
  if(iter %% 20 == 0){
      cat("Iteration: ", iter)
      print("Weights: ")
      print(unlist(self$w))
  }

  }
  }
  , predict = function(X){
      X <- cbind(-1,X) #add bias
      preds <- c()
      for(i in 1:nrow(X)){
          preds[i] <- self$forward(X[i,])
      }
  return(preds)
  }
```

```
      )
   )
```

As we can see, there are not a lot of changes with respect to the previous code, the main action happening on the backward step.

Multi-layer perceptron

Like pancakes, neural networks are made to be stacked with each other. We can make the output of a layer the input of the next layer, called a **hidden layer**. This hidden layer consists of a linear combination of the inputs to which an activation function is applied. This creates a new hidden vector which we can take as an input for the following hidden layer, on each step recombining the outputs from the previous layer by some weights and applying an activation function.

Let's start by introducing the sigmoid function, which will be useful later:

```
library(R6)

sigmoid <- function(x){
  1/(1+exp(-x))
}
```

The skeleton of the class is now:

```
MLP <- R6Class("MLP",
                    public = list(
                      dim = NULL,
                      n_iter = NULL,
                      learning_rate = NULL,
                      hidden_layer_size=NULL,
                      Wih = NULL,
                      Who = NULL,
                      a = NULL,
                      initialize = function(learning_rate = 0.3,
                                      n_iter=NA,
                                      dim=NA,
                                      hidden_layer_size=NA){
                    #INITIALIZATION CODE
                  }
                  , forward = function(x){
                      #Input: training vector
                      #Output: Class
                  }
                  , backward = function(t,y,X){
                      # Input: Target, prediction and matrix of
```

```
    training examples
                                # No output, gradients are modified in the class

                    }
                    , train = function(X,t){
                      # Run the training loop: forward and backward
propagation for n_iter
                    }
                    , predict = function(X){
                        # Call to the forward function for all training
examples
                    }
                )
    )
```

The forward step is usually the simplest, which in our case is:

```
    , forward = function(x){
                            h <- as.matrix(x)%*%self$Wih
                            self$a <- sigmoid(h)
                            y <- sigmoid(self$a %*% self$Who) #Output of the
network
                            return(y)
                    }
```

The backward step is the tricky part here. We have one error component, coming from the derivative of the loss function with respect to the last component. This is called `layer2_delta` in the code. The other component comes from the derivative with respect to the weights on the first layer, called `layer1_delta`. These are the derivatives that need to be evaluated in the corresponding points, namely X for the case of `layer1_delta` and the output a of the activation function for `layer2_delta`.

```
    , backward = function(t,y,X){
                            # Compute the error in the output layer
                            layer2_error <- t-y
                            layer2_delta <- (layer2_error)*(y*(1-y))

                            #Compute the error in the input layer
                            layer1_error <- layer2_delta %*% t(self$Who)
                            layer1_delta <- layer1_error*self$a*(1-self$a)
                            # Adjustments of the weights
                            layer1_adjustment <- t(X) %*% layer1_delta
                            layer2_adjustment <- t(self$a) %*% layer2_delta
                            self$Wih <-
self$Wih+self$learning_rate*layer1_adjustment
                            self$Who <-
```

```
self$Who+self$learning_rate*layer2_adjustment
                     }
```

The other functions are easier to complete. For completeness, the full code is included here:

```
MLP <- R6Class("MLP",
                    public = list(
                        dim = NULL,
                        n_iter = NULL,
                        learning_rate = NULL,
                        hidden_layer_size=NULL,
                        Wih = NULL,
                        Who = NULL,
                        a = NULL,
                        initialize = function(learning_rate = 0.3,
                                              n_iter=NA,
                                              dim=NA,
                                              hidden_layer_size=NA){
                        self$dim <- dim
                        self$n_iter <- n_iter
                        self$learning_rate <- learning_rate
                        self$hidden_layer_size <- hidden_layer_size
                        self$Wih <-
matrix(runif(self$hidden_layer_size*self$dim),
                                               ncol =
self$hidden_layer_size)
                        self$Who <-
matrix(runif((self$hidden_layer_size)), ncol = 1)
                        self$a <-
matrix(runif(self$hidden_layer_size*self$dim), ncol = self$dim)
                        }
                    , forward = function(x){
                        h <- as.matrix(x)%*%self$Wih
                        self$a <- sigmoid(h)
                        y <- sigmoid(self$a %*% self$Who) #Output of the
network
                        return(y)
                        }
                    , backward = function(t,y,X){
                        # Compute the error in the output layer
                        layer2_error <- t-y
                        layer2_delta <- (layer2_error)*(y*(1-y))

                        #Compute the error in the input layer
                        layer1_error <- layer2_delta %*% t(self$Who)
                        layer1_delta <- layer1_error*self$a*(1-self$a)
                        # Adjustments of the weights
```

```
                              layer1_adjustment <- t(X) %*% layer1_delta
                              layer2_adjustment <- t(self$a) %*% layer2_delta
                              self$Wih <-
        self$Wih+self$learning_rate*layer1_adjustment
                              self$Who <-
        self$Who+self$learning_rate*layer2_adjustment

                    }
                  , train = function(X,t){
                    n_examples <- nrow(X)
                    for(iter in 1:self$n_iter){
                      preds <- self$forward(X)
                      self$backward(t,preds, X)
                      if(iter %% 1000 == 0){
                        cat("Iteration: ", iter,"\n")
                      }
                    }
                  }
                  , predict = function(X){
                    preds <- self$forward(X)
                    return(preds)
                  }
                )
        )
```

Let's try our network in the OR function, which as we saw, is linearly separable:

```
x1 <- c(0,0,1,1)
x2 <- c(0,1,0,1)
t <- c(0,1,1,1)
X <- as.matrix(data.frame(x1=x1, x2=x2))
```

Now, let's generate the predicted labels:

```
clf <- MLP$new(n_iter=5000,dim=ncol(X), hidden_layer_size=4)
clf$train(X,t)
clf$predict(X)
```

Well, that's all very nice, but certainly not much of an advantage, right? We already knew that this simple training example was correctly solved by the perceptron.

To really go one step further, let's consider the following data (the xor) function:

```
xor <- data.frame(x1=c(0,0,1,1), x2=c(0,1,0,1), t = c(0,1,1,0))
clf$train(xor[,1:2],xor[,3])
clf$predict(xor[,1:2])
```

We know that this is not linearly separable:

```
library(ggplot2)
grid_size <- 1e2
grid <- data.frame(V1=0,V2=0)
base <- seq(0,1,1/grid_size)
```

Let's generate a grid to which we will apply the decision function:

```
for(j in 1:grid_size){
 V1 <- rep(base[j],grid_size+1)
 V2 <- base
 tmp <- data.frame(V1=V1,V2=V2)
 grid <- rbind(tmp,grid)
}
```

Now, let's finally plot the evaluation of this function on the grid:

```
grid$z <- with(grid,clf$predict(cbind(V1,V2)))
ggplot(grid,aes(x=V1,y=V2))+geom_tile(aes(fill=z))+theme_bw()
```

We see that the multi-layer perceptron does a better job on this data, and is able to correctly guess the separation boundary between these two regions:

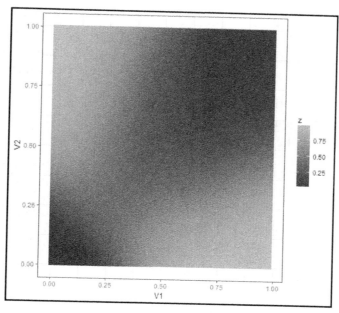

Implementing a RNN

Let's go to the most important part of this chapter. Implementing our recurrent neural network with our bare hands. We show two different implementations, the first one using R6 classes, which we find could be more useful for using in your projects, since it is more portable. The second implementation we show closely follows sample code used in Andrej Karpathy's blog post for a minimal character-level recurrent neural network cited previously.

Implementation as an R6 class

First, let's show the skeleton of this class. We need a number of functions here. First, we need to import the R6 package and create two auxiliary functions:

```
library(R6)
set.seed(1234)
softmax <- function(x){
  xt <- exp(x-max(x))
  return(xt/sum(xt))
}
zeros_like <- function(M){
  return(matrix(0,dim(as.matrix(M))[1],dim(as.matrix(M))[2]))
}
```

This will come in handy during the code to calculate the *softmax* and initialize matrices with the correct sizes. As before, our program needs the following basic functions:

- Forward propagation
- Backward propagation
- A sample from the obtained probability distribution
- Train the model

The structure of the class should look like:

```
RNN <- R6Class("RNN",
        public = list(
        hidden_size = NULL,
        vocab_size = NULL,
        learning_rate = NULL,
        U = NULL,
        V = NULL,
        W = NULL,
        seq_length = NULL,
        chars = NULL,
```

```
          n_iter = NULL,
          initialize = function(hidden_size = NA, vocab_size = NA,
                      chars=NA, n_iter=100, seq_length=NA,
learning_rate=0.01){
          }
          , forward_step = function(input_sample){
              ## Takes one column vector and returns the softmax output
          }
          , bptt = function(inputs,targets,s_prev){
              seq_size <- length(inputs) #total length of the sequence
              loss <- 0
              for(idx in 1:seq_size){
                # Forward pass: Update the hidden state and predict
                # Backward pass: updates using the gradient
                  for(j in length(inputs):1){
                      ## derivatives of error vs output
                      }
              }
              return(list("loss"=loss, "dU"=dU, "dW"=dW, "dV"=dV,
"hs"=hs[length(inputs)-1]))
          }
          ,   sample_char <- function(h, seed_ix, n){
          ## generate a sample from the model
          ## given a hidden state and an initial seed
              }
          , train = function(text){
              ## Main training loop with Adagrad updates
              }
      )
  )
```

The most interesting is the `bptt` function, so let us describe it in more detail. When the inputs from the environment are received, in this case, a chunk of text, we will loop through every character of this chunk and generate predictions for the following states given the present state and the value of the hidden state from the previous iteration. Once we traverse the input chunk, we need to calculate the updates for the gradients in reverse order. This is done in the back propagation part of this function.

We observed better performance with Adagrad instead of stochastic gradient descent, which should be implemented on the final part, in the `train` function.

The full code is:

```
library(R6)
set.seed(1234)
softmax <- function(x){
  xt <- exp(x-max(x))
```

```
    return(xt/sum(xt))
}
zeros_like <- function(M){
  return(matrix(0,dim(as.matrix(M))[1],dim(as.matrix(M))[2]))
}
RNN <- R6Class("RNN",
                 public = list(
                    hidden_size = NULL,
                    vocab_size = NULL,
                    learning_rate = NULL,
                    U = NULL,
                    V = NULL,
                    W = NULL,
                    seq_length = NULL,
                    chars = NULL,
                    n_iter = NULL,
                    initialize = function(hidden_size = NA, vocab_size = NA,
chars=NA, n_iter=100, seq_length=NA, learning_rate=0.01){
                        self$hidden_size <- hidden_size
                        self$n_iter <- n_iter
                        self$learning_rate <- learning_rate
                        self$seq_length <- seq_length
                        self$vocab_size <- as.numeric(vocab_size)
                        self$chars <- chars
                        self$U <- matrix(rnorm(hidden_size*vocab_size)*0.01,
nrow=self$hidden_size) # input to hidden
                        self$W <- matrix(rnorm(hidden_size*hidden_size)*0.01,
nrow=self$hidden_size) # hidden to hidden
                        self$V <- matrix(rnorm(vocab_size*hidden_size)*0.01,
nrow=self$vocab_size) # hidden to output
                    }
                    , forward_step = function(input_sample){
                        ## Takes one column vector and returns probabilities
                        x <- input_sample
                        s <- tanh(self$U%*%x+self$W%*%self$s)
                        o <- softmax(self$V%*%self$s)
                        return(list("pred"=o,"state"=s))
                    }
                    , bptt = function(inputs,targets,s_prev){
                        seq_size <- length(inputs) #total length of the sequence
                        xs <- lapply(vector('list',seq_size), function(i)
matrix(0,self$vocab_size, 1))
                        hs <- lapply(vector('list',seq_size), function(i)
matrix(0,self$hidden_size, 1))
                        ys <- lapply(vector('list',seq_size), function(i)
matrix(0,self$vocab_size, 1))
                        ps <- lapply(vector('list',seq_size), function(i)
matrix(0,self$vocab_size,1))
```

```
loss <- 0
for(idx in 1:seq_size){
  xs[[idx]] <- matrix(0,self$vocab_size,1)
  xs[[idx]][inputs[[idx]]] = 1
  ## Update the hidden state
  if(idx==1){
    hs[[idx]] <-
tanh(self$U%*%xs[[idx]]+self$W%*%s_prev)
  }
  else{
    hs[[idx]] <-
tanh(self$U%*%xs[[idx]]+self$W%*%hs[[(idx-1)]])
  }
  ## calculate the probabilities for the next character
  ys[[idx]] <- self$V%*%hs[[idx]]
  ps[[idx]] <- softmax(ys[[idx]])
  ## Cross-entropy loss
  loss <- loss-log(ps[[idx]][targets[idx], 1])
  # Calculate gradients
  dU <- zeros_like(self$U)
  dW <- zeros_like(self$W)
  dV <- zeros_like(self$V)
  dhnext <- zeros_like(s_prev)
  for(j in length(inputs):1){
    ## Gradient of the error vs output
    dy <- ps[[j]]
    dy[targets[j]] <- dy[targets[j]]-1
    dV <- dV+dy%*%t(hs[[j]])
    dh <- t(self$V)%*%dy + dhnext
    ## backprop through the tanh
    dhraw <- (1 - hs[[j]] * hs[[j]]) * dh
    ## derivative of the error between input and hidden
layer
    dU <- dU+dhraw%*%t(xs[[j]])
    if(j==1){
      dW <- dW+dhraw%*%t(s_prev)
    }
    else{
      dW <- dW+dhraw%*%t(hs[[(j-1)]])
    }
    dhnext <- t(self$W)%*%dhraw
  }
}
return(list("loss"=loss, "dU"=dU, "dW"=dW, "dV"=dV,
"hs"=hs[length(inputs)-1]))
}
,
sample_char = function(h, seed_ix, n){
```

```r
# Generate a sequence of characters given a seed and a
hidden state
x <- matrix(0,self$vocab_size, 1)
x[seed_ix] <- 1
ixes <- c()
for(t in 1:n){
  h <- tanh(self$U%*%x+self$W%*%h)
  y <- self$V%*%h
  p <- exp(y)/sum(exp(y)) #softmax
  ix <- sample(self$chars,size=1, replace=T, prob=p)
  x <- matrix(0,self$vocab_size,1)
  x[which(chars==ix)] <- 1
  ixes[t] <- ix
}
return(ixes)
}
, train = function(text){
  n <- 1
  p <- 1
  mU <- zeros_like(self$U)
  mW <- zeros_like(self$W)
  mV <- zeros_like(self$V)
  # memory variables for Adagrad
  smooth_loss = -log(1.0/self$vocab_size)*self$seq_length
  # loss at iteration 0
  for(n in 1:self$n_iter){
    #
    if(p + self$seq_length + 1 >= length(text) || n == 1){
      # reset RNN memory
      ## h_old is the previous hidden state of RNN
      h_old <- matrix(0,self$hidden_size, 1)
      # go from start of data
      p <- 1
    }
    inputs <-
unlist(lapply(text[p:(p+self$seq_length)],function(c){which(self$chars==c)}
))
    targets <-
unlist(lapply(text[(p+1):(p+self$seq_length+1)],function(c){which(self$char
s==c)}))
    # See what the model is doing from time to time
    if(n %% 100 == 0){
      txt <- self$sample_char(h_old, inputs[[1]], 200)
      ## Find the line breaks
      line_breaks <- which(txt=="\n")
      if(length(line_breaks)<2){
        print(txt)
      }
```

```r
      else{
        for(ix in 2:(length(line_breaks-1))){
          first_ix <- line_breaks[ix-1]+1
          last_ix <- line_breaks[ix]-1
          print(paste(txt[first_ix:last_ix], collapse=""))
        }
      }
      smooth_loss = smooth_loss*0.99+loss*0.01
      print('---- sample -----')
      cat("Iteration number: ",n,  "\n")
      cat("Loss: ", smooth_loss)
    }
    tmp <- self$bptt(inputs, targets, h_old)
    loss <- unlist(tmp$loss)
    dU <- unlist(tmp$dU)
    dW <- unlist(tmp$dW)
    dV <- unlist(tmp$dV)
    h_old <- unlist(tmp$hs)
    ## Time to update the Adagrad weights
    mU <- mU+dU**2
    self$U <- self$U-self$learning_rate * dU / sqrt(mU +
1e-8)

    mW <- mW+dW**2
    self$W <- self$W-self$learning_rate * dW / sqrt(mW +
1e-8)

    mV <- mV+dV**2
    self$V <- self$V-self$learning_rate * dV / sqrt(mV +
1e-8)

    p <- p+self$seq_length
    n <- n+1
  }
  return(1)
}
)
)
```

There is certainly some work to be done here. For instance, you can refactor the part of the forward pass to use the `forward_step` function explicitly. We leave that as an exercise.

To test your code, you can use the list of male and female names (see the *Exercises* section). We show how to do this if we use the list for female names (after removing the header information manually):

```r
library(readr)
library(stringr)
library(purrr)
library(tokenizers)
```

```
data <- read_lines("./data/female.txt")
text <- data %>%
    str_to_lower() %>%
    str_c(collapse = "\n") %>%
    tokenize_characters(strip_non_alphanum = FALSE, simplify = TRUE)
chars <- text %>% unique
test <- RNN$new(hidden_size = 100,
                vocab_size = length(chars),
                chars=chars,
                n_iter=100,
                seq_length=25,
                learning_rate=0.01)
test$train(text)
```

You can use your own data; it simply needs to be a text file.

While training your models with your own data, be careful with what you are passing as input, always remember, *garbage in, garbage out*. Insert some logs or print statements here and there, so that you can see what your network doing.

Implementation without R6

In this section, we include the implementation of the same basic recurrent neural network without using R6 classes. First, some imports and setting the seed:

```
library(readr)
library(stringr)
library(purrr)
library(tokenizers)
set.seed(1234)
```

We introduce an auxiliary function to initialize to zeros a matrix with the shape of a matrix, M:

```
zeros_like <- function(M){
 return(matrix(0,dim(as.matrix(M))[1],dim(as.matrix(M))[2]))
}
```

We also need the softmax function:

```
softmax <- function(x){
 xt <- exp(x-max(x))
 return(xt/sum(xt))
}
```

We will use this for testing the female names data (see the *Exercises* section):

```
data <- read_lines("./data/female.txt")
```

And do some preprocessing:

```
text <- data %>%
  str_to_lower() %>%
  str_c(collapse = "\n") %>%
  tokenize_characters(strip_non_alphanum = FALSE, simplify = TRUE)
```

We set up the characters of our vocabulary. This is required to do the one-hot encoding of each input data:

```
chars <- text %>% unique
chars
```

Now, we go to the main part of the program. Besides the initializations, notice that we define a `lossFun` which includes the forward steps and backpropagation through time:

```
library(readr)
library(stringr)
library(purrr)
library(tokenizers)

set.seed(1234)

zeros_like <- function(M){
  return(matrix(0,dim(as.matrix(M))[1],dim(as.matrix(M))[2]))
}


softmax <- function(x){
  xt <- exp(x-max(x))
  return(xt/sum(xt))
}
data <- read_lines("./data/female.txt")
head(data)


text <- data %>%
  str_to_lower() %>%
  str_c(collapse = "\n") %>%
  tokenize_characters(strip_non_alphanum = FALSE, simplify = TRUE)


chars <- text %>% unique
chars
```

```r
# hyperparameters
hidden_size = 100 # size of hidden layer of neurons
seq_length = 10 # number of steps to unroll the RNN for
learning_rate = 1e-1
vocab_size = length(chars)


U <- matrix(rnorm(hidden_size*vocab_size)*0.01, nrow=hidden_size) # input
to hidden
W <- matrix(rnorm(hidden_size*hidden_size)*0.01, nrow=hidden_size) # hidden
to hidden
V <- matrix(rnorm(vocab_size*hidden_size)*0.01, nrow=vocab_size) # hidden
to output
bh <- matrix(0,hidden_size, 1) # hidden bias
by <- matrix(0,vocab_size, 1) # output bias


lossFun <- function(inputs,targets,prev_hidden){
  tot <- length(inputs) #total sequence length
  xs <- lapply(vector('list',tot), function(i) matrix(0,vocab_size, 1))
  hs <- lapply(vector('list',tot), function(i) matrix(0,hidden_size, 1))
  ys <- lapply(vector('list',tot), function(i) matrix(0,vocab_size, 1))
  ps <- lapply(vector('list',tot), function(i) matrix(0,vocab_size,1))
  loss <- 0
  for(idx in 1:tot){
    xs[[idx]] <- matrix(0,vocab_size,1)
    xs[[idx]][inputs[[idx]]] = 1

    ## update the hidden state
    if(idx==1){
      hs[[idx]] <- tanh(U%*%xs[[idx]]+W%*%h_old+bh)
    }
    else{
      hs[[idx]] <- tanh(U%*%xs[[idx]]+W%*%hs[[(idx-1)]]+bh)
    }
    ## Get char probabilities
    ys[[idx]] <- V%*%hs[[idx]] + by
    ps[[idx]] <- softmax(ys[[idx]])
    ## Loss function (cross-entropy here)
    loss <- loss-log(ps[[idx]][targets[idx], 1])
    # Initialize the gradients
    dU <- zeros_like(U)
    dW <- zeros_like(W)
    dV <- zeros_like(V)
    dbh <- zeros_like(bh)
    dby <- zeros_like(by)
    dhnext <- zeros_like(h_old)
    # Here comes the backprop loop
```

```
    for(j in length(inputs):1){
      # Output vs loss
      dy <- ps[[j]]
      dy[targets[j]] <- dy[targets[j]]-1
      dV <- dV+dy%*%t(hs[[j]])
      dby <- dby+dy
      ## Hidden layer
      dh <- t(V)%*%dy + dhnext
      dh_raw <- (1 - hs[[j]] * hs[[j]]) * dh
      dbh <- dbh+dh_raw
      dU <- dU+dh_raw%*%t(xs[[j]])
      if(j==1){
        dW <- dW+dh_raw%*%t(h_old)
      }
      else{
        dW <- dW+dh_raw%*%t(hs[[(j-1)]])
      }
      dhnext <- t(W)%*%dh_raw
    }
  }
  return(list("loss"=loss, "dU"=dU, "dW"=dW, "dV"=dV, "dbh"=dbh, "dby"=dby,
"hs"=hs[length(inputs)-1]))
}


## Sample a few chars given a hidden state and a seed
sample_char <- function(h, seed_ix, n){
  x <- matrix(0,vocab_size, 1)
  x[seed_ix] <- 1
  ixes <- c()
  for(t in 1:n){
    h <- tanh(U%*%x+W%*%h+bh)
    y <- V%*%h+by
    p <- exp(y)/sum(exp(y)) #softmax
    ix <- sample(chars,size=1, replace=T, prob=p)
    x <- matrix(0,vocab_size,1)
    x[which(chars==ix)] <- 1
    ixes[t] <- ix
  }
  return(ixes)
}


n <- 1
p <- 1

mU <- zeros_like(U)
mW <- zeros_like(W)
```

```
mV <- zeros_like(V)
mbh <- zeros_like(bh)
mby <- zeros_like(by) # memory variables for Adagrad
smooth_loss = -log(1.0/vocab_size)*seq_length # loss at iteration 0

while(T){
  if(p + seq_length + 1 >= length(data) || n == 1){
    # reset RNN memory
    ## h_old is the hidden state of RNN
    h_old <- matrix(0,hidden_size, 1)
    # go from the start of the data
    p <- 1
  }
  inputs <-
unlist(sapply(text[p:(p+seq_length)],function(c){which(chars==c)}))
  targets <-
unlist(sapply(text[(p+1):(p+seq_length+1)],function(c){which(chars==c)}))
  # Check what the model is doing from time to time
  if(n %% 100 == 0){
    txt <- sample_char(h_old, inputs[[1]], 200)
    ## Find line breaks
    line_breaks <- which(txt=="\n")
    if(length(line_breaks)<2){
      print(txt)
    }
    else{
      for(ix in 2:(length(line_breaks-1))){
        first_ix <- line_breaks[ix-1]+1
        last_ix <- line_breaks[ix]-1
        print(paste(txt[first_ix:last_ix], collapse=""))
      }
    }
    smooth_loss = smooth_loss*0.99+loss*0.01
    print('---- sample -----')
    cat("Iteration number: ",n, "\n")
    cat("Loss: ", smooth_loss)
  }
  tmp <- lossFun(inputs, targets, h_old)
  loss <- unlist(tmp$loss)
  dU <- unlist(tmp$dU)
  dW <- unlist(tmp$dW)
  dV <- unlist(tmp$dV)
  dbh <- unlist(tmp$dbh)
  dby <- unlist(tmp$dby)
  h_old <- unlist(tmp$hs)
  ## Weight updates for Adagrad

  mU <- mU+dU**2
```

```
U <- U-learning_rate * dU / sqrt(mU + 1e-8)
mW <- mW+dW**2
W <- W-learning_rate * dW / sqrt(mW + 1e-8)
mV <- mV+dV**2
V <- V-learning_rate * dV / sqrt(mV + 1e-8)
mbh <- mbh+mbh**2
bh <- bh-learning_rate * dbh / sqrt(mbh + 1e-8)
mby <- mby+dby**2
by <- by-learning_rate * dby / sqrt(mby + 1e-8)

p <- p+seq_length
n <- n+1
}
```

What does this recurrent neural network produce? In the beginning, we get the following female names:

```
[1] "iaiaaan"
[1] "aannaeinraaniaraeinareanaeaaraana"
[1] "iainii"
[1] "laeoda"
[1] "arineaeia"
[1] "rdiiaai"
[1] "eiaa"
[1] "irineaaasrnaaaaaalaiiaaiaiiaranaxiaaaannnaiiorieiida"
[1] "naiiaaiaaialiaraaaaannaian"
[1] "aaaaieaiaain"
[1] "nad"
[1] "iiaaeaeaianiaa"
[1] "---- sample -----"
Iteration number: 100
```

After some time, the network starts to make sense of the data:

```
[1] "anna"
[1] "annanianinbnatarmadnanannannnablantd"
[1] "antsnamannd"
[1] "iniaina"
[1] "anta"
[1] "alnaenalnalna"
[1] "annilinnina"
[1] "anma"
[1] "bna"
[1] "anganna"
[1] "alnaniannnna"
[1] "iriannannennandana"
[1] "anyoa"
[1] "annannllynaenpanda"
```

```
[1] "anedaannna"
[1] "anna"
[1] "---- sample -----"
Iteration number: 700
```

Note how really amazing this is. After only 700 iterations, you start rediscovering female names, and generate a few real-sounding names (like `anyoa`). All this is achieved from the character level. The network has no idea about words, nor language. It is able to create those names from statistical dependencies on the input data only.

What else can we do? I tried the same code on the LaTeX version of my PhD thesis. After a few thousand iterations, it learns to do the imports of the packages correctly. A bit further ahead, it starts to write small words in English. You can try it with other data; see the *Exercises* section for some suggestions.

RNN without derivatives — the cross-entropy method

We will replace the backward propagation part on the preceding neural network with a Monte Carlo algorithm, called the **cross-entropy method**. This is a general-purpose algorithm introduced by Reuven Rubinstein which is quite helpful in many cases, especially for rare event simulation. It has been proven efficient for many reinforcement learning tasks, so why not give it a try?

The method consists of two parts:

1. Generate a random data sample (trajectories, vectors) according to a specified mechanism.
2. Update the parameters of the random mechanism based on the data to produce a *better* sample in the next iteration. This step involves minimizing the cross-entropy or Kullback–Leibler divergence.

Let's first illustrate the situation with a small sample code. Suppose we want to minimize the function:

```
# the function we need to maximize
f <- function(theta){
 reward = -sum((solution - theta)**2)
 return(reward)
}
```

The maximum of this function, as a function of `theta`, is reached when `theta==solution`.

Let's fix a value for `solution` as the vector:

```
solution <- c(0.5, 0.1, -0.3)
```

And set up some initial parameters:

```
dim_theta <- 3
theta_mean <- matrix(0,dim_theta,1)
theta_std <- diag(dim_theta)
```

The cross-entropy method we will use works as follows:

- Generate some sample solutions using an initial estimate for mean and standard deviation of the parameters.
- Calculate as many as `batch_size` of those (where `batch_size` is a hyper-parameter).
- Consider only a fraction of them, called the elite fraction (`elite_frac`). This is another hyper-parameter.
- Get the top `elite_frac` of those, that means, those generated sample solutions that gave the highest reward in terms of the function we want to maximize.
- Find the mean and covariance of those parameters to generate new candidate solutions.

The following code example shows how to implement the logic described previously:

```
cem <- function(f, n_iter, theta_mean, theta_std, batch_size=25,
elite_frac=0.2){
 for(it in 1:n_iter){
 # Get a sample using the previous parameters
 thetas <- matrix(mvrnorm(n=batch_size*dim_theta, mu= theta_mean,
Sigma=theta_std), ncol = dim_theta)
 rewards <- apply(thetas,1,f)
 # Now choose the best
 n_elite <- as.integer(batch_size * elite_frac)
 elite_inds <- sort(rewards, decreasing = T, index.return=T)$ix[1:n_elite]
 elite_thetas <- thetas[elite_inds,]
 # Update theta_mean, theta_std
 theta_mean <- apply(elite_thetas, 2,mean)
 theta_std <- 0.01*diag(dim_theta)+0.99*cov(elite_thetas)
 }
 return(theta_mean)
}
```

We call our function:

```
cem(f,300, theta_mean, theta_std)
```

And we get a very reasonable approximation of those values, in only a few iterations.

For the text generation problem, we need to gather together our matrices, self$U, self$V, self$W, into a big vector, theta, run the forward pass of the network, and calculate the negative of the log loss. So, we have a function that maps our vector into a scalar value, which is the same situation as shown prior. The train function is the only one that gets modified, and will look as follows:

```
train = function(text){
                n <- 1
                p <- 1
                smooth_loss = -log(1.0/self$vocab_size)*self$seq_length
# loss at iteration 0
                for(n in 1:self$n_iter){
                  if(p + self$seq_length + 1 >= length(text) || n == 1){
                    # reset RNN memory
                    ## s_prev is the hidden state of RNN
                    s_prev <- matrix(0,self$hidden_size, 1)
                    # go from start of data
                    p <- 1
                  }
                  inputs <-
unlist(lapply(text[p:(p+self$seq_length)],function(c){which(self$chars==c)}
))
                  targets <-
unlist(lapply(text[(p+1):(p+self$seq_length+1)],function(c){which(self$char
s==c)}))
                  if(n %% 100 == 0){
                    txt <- self$sample_char(s_prev, inputs[[1]], 200)
                    ## Find the \n in the string
                    line_breaks <- which(txt=="\n")
                    if(length(line_breaks)<2){
                      print(txt)
                    }
                    else{
                      for(ix in 2:(length(line_breaks-1))){
                        first_ix <- line_breaks[ix-1]+1
                        last_ix <- line_breaks[ix]-1
                        print(paste(txt[first_ix:last_ix], collapse=""))
                      }
                    }
                    print('---- sample -----')
                    cat("Iteration number: ",n, "\n")
```

```
            cat("Loss: ", smooth_loss)
          }
          ## UPDATES
          theta_m <- c(as.vector(self$U), as.vector(self$V),
as.vector(self$W))
          new_m <- cem(-self$forward, theta_m,
diag(length(theta_m))*0.01)
          self$U <-
as.matrix(theta_m[1:hidden_size*vocab_size],nrow=self$hidden_size)
          self$W <-
as.matrix(theta_m[(hidden_size*vocab_size+1):(hidden_size*(vocab_size+hidde
n_size)+1)],
                                        nrow=self$hidden_size)
          self$V <-
as.matrix(theta_m[(hidden_size*(vocab_size+hidden_size)+1):length(theta_m)]
, nrow=self$vocab_size) # hidden to output
          loss <- self$forward(inputs,targets,s_prev)
          p <- p+self$seq_length
          n <- n+1
        }
        return(1)
      }
```

You can try this on your own! The results are comparable, although note that it takes much longer to run! This is, unfortunately, the situation with many of the algorithms relying on stochastic optimization, whether Monte Carlo or evolutionary algorithms. However, often the waiting time is worth it, because they are able to avoid local extrema and have at least a high probability of reaching the optimum.

With the preceding code, you have a good template to start trying different evolutionary algorithms.

RNN using Keras

In this section, we introduce an example using Keras. Keras is possibly the highest-level API for deep learning (again, at the time of writing, in this rapidly changing world of deep learning). This is very useful when you need to do production-ready models quite quickly, but is unfortunately sometimes not that great for learning, as everything is hidden away from you. Since, ideally, by the time you reach this section, an expert in recurrent neural networks, we can present you how to create a similar model.

Before that, let's introduce a simple benchmark model. Something that comes to mind when we speak about the memory of a neural network is the following, well, what if I had sufficient storage to calculate the conditional probabilities and simulate text generation as a Markov process, where the state variable is the observed text? We will implement this benchmark model to see how it compares in text generation quality with recurrent neural networks.

A simple benchmark implementation

Let's create a simple benchmark implementation and simulate text generation as a Markov chain. The idea is the following, we will estimate the probability of character c appearing after history h has been observed, where h has a fixed length. This length is called **memory**. For example, if we have a tiny corpus consisting of:

```
"My name is Pablo"
```

And we fix a memory length of 4, we get a training set that looks like this:

h	c
My n	a
y na	m
nam	e

Our task is to estimate the conditional probability distribution:

$$\mathbb{P}(c \mid h)$$

This conditional probability is obtained simply by estimating the number of times c appears after h, divided by the number of times history h appears.

The goal of this chapter is to build a benchmark model. We should clarify what we mean, as there is no *golden standard* for assessing performance in generative models. The way we will evaluate the model is by looking at the quality of the text generated, for which we need information about the context of the problem, namely, the corpus we want to learn to generate text from.

For this example, we will use the text of *Alice in Wonderland*, the book by Lewis Carroll, which is available online thanks to Project Gutenberg. You can find it on their website: `https://www.gutenberg.org/`.

We start by loading some libraries:

```
library(readr)
library(stringr)
library(purrr)
library(tokenizers)
library(dplyr)
```

Now, we load the data (available on the book's website), and set up a memory length of 5:

```
orig <- read_lines("./data/alice.txt")
maxlen <- 2
```

Next, we should clean our text from newlines and convert everything to lowercase for simplicity:

```
text <- orig %>%
  str_to_lower() %>%
  str_c(collapse = "\n") %>%
  tokenize_characters(strip_non_alphanum = FALSE, simplify = TRUE)
```

We set the variable `chars` as our set of tokens:

```
chars <- text %>% unique %>% sort
```

We now initialize an empty data frame and define a function to convert the tokenized vector input into a string:

```
records <- data.frame()
vec2str <- function(history){
 history <- toString(history)
 history <- str_replace_all(history,",","")
 history <- str_replace_all(history," ","")
 history <- str_replace_all(history,"\n"," ")
 history
 }
```

Now, we need to loop through the history and store in the records data frame:

```
idxs <- seq(1, length(text) - max_length - 1, by=3)
for(i in idxs){
 history <- text[i:(i+max_length-1)]
 next_char <- text[i+max_length]
 history <- vec2str(history)
 records <- rbind(data.frame(history=history, next_char=next_char),
records)
 tot_rows <- length(idxs)
}
```

Finally, we calculate the conditional probabilities:

$$\mathbb{P}(c \mid h)$$

Introduced previously. This can be done very easily using the dplyr package, as follows:

```
library(dplyr)
tot_histories <- records %>%
                 group_by(history) %>%
                 summarize(total_h=n())
tot_histories_char <- records %>%
                      group_by(history, next_char) %>%
                      summarize(total_h_c=n())
probas <- left_join(tot_histories, tot_histories_char)
probas$prob <- probas$total_h_c/probas$total_h
```

Now, we are ready to start generating text! We define a text generating function that will sample the next character conditional on the history:

```
generate_next <- function(h){
  sub_df <- probas%>%filter(history==h)
  if(nrow(sub_df)>0){
    prob_vector <- sub_df %>% select(prob)%>%as.matrix %>%c()
    char_vector <- sub_df %>% select(next_char)%>%as.matrix %>%c()
    char_vector <- as.vector(char_vector)
    sample(char_vector,size=1,prob=prob_vector)
  }
}
```

The preceding function helps us sample characters from the distribution we estimated.

With the following code, we can generate words of different lengths, to make it more interesting:

```
n_iter <- 100
for(iter in 1:n_iter){
  # Generate random initialization
  generated <- " "
  start_index <- sample(1:(length(text) - maxlen), size = 1)
  h <- text[start_index:(start_index + maxlen - 1)]
  h <- vec2str(h)
  random_len <- sample(5:10,1)
  for(i in 1:random_len){
    c <- generate_next(h)
    h <- paste0(h,c)
    generated <- str_c(generated,c)
    h <- substr(h,i,i+maxlen)
  }
  cat(generated)
  cat("\n")
}
```

Generating new text from old

Let's compare our simple, Markov chain model benchmark against LSTM networks. You can use the implementation we used earlier in this chapter. We will show how to use the Keras API for this task, as we did in the previous chapter.

We will illustrate this with an example close to one of the authors' hearts, generating names in Spanish.

First, we should load the required libraries:

```
library(keras)
library(readr)
library(stringr)
library(purrr)
library(tokenizers)
```

Then, define a sampling function based on the probabilities we will estimate:

```
sample_mod <- function(preds, temperature = 0.8){
  preds <- log(preds)/temperature
  exp_preds <- exp(preds)
  preds <- exp_preds/sum(exp(preds))
  rmultinom(1, 1, preds) %>%
```

```
    as.integer() %>%
    which.max()
}
```

Strictly speaking, we do not estimate probabilities, rather some score between 0 and 1 which we can understand as such. The point is that this score will help us generate text, and the score has the same order as the real probabilities. A higher score equates to higher probability.

Now, we read the file and do some parsing. This is very similar to before:

```
orig <- read_lines("./data/Spanish.txt")
text <- orig %>%
    str_to_lower() %>%
    str_c(collapse = "\n") %>%
    tokenize_characters(strip_non_alphanum = FALSE, simplify = TRUE)
```

We define the vocabulary, that is, the collection of tokens in our text:

```
chars <- text %>%
    str_c(collapse="\n")%>%
    tokenize_characters(simplify=TRUE) %>%
    unique %>% sort
chars
 [1] "a" "á" "à" "b" "c" "d" "e" "é" "f" "g" "h" "i" "í" "j" "l" "m" "n" "ñ"
"o" "ó" "p" "q" "r" "s" "t" "u"
[27] "ú" "v" "x" "y" "z"
```

We keep the accentuated vowels, as they are part of the language. Next, we set up the window size and cut the text into overlapping sequences of that size:

```
max_length <- 5
dataset <- map(
 seq(1, length(text) - max_length - 1, by = 3),
 ~list(name = text[.x:(.x + max_length - 1)], next_char = text[.x +
max_length])
)
dataset <- transpose(dataset)
```

We use one-hot vectorization to encode our data into numerical inputs for the neural network that we will build using the keras library:

```
# One-hot vectorization
X <- array(0, dim = c(length(dataset$name), max_length, length(chars)))
y <- array(0, dim = c(length(dataset$name), length(chars)))
```

Finally, we set up the training set:

```
for(i in 1:length(dataset$name)){
    X[i,,] <- sapply(chars, function(x){
    as.integer(x == dataset$name[[i]])
    })
  y[i,] <- as.integer(chars == dataset$next_char[[i]])
  }
```

Then, we define the architecture of our network:

```
model <- keras_model_sequential()
model %>%
  layer_lstm(128, input_shape = c(max_length, length(chars))) %>%
  layer_dense(length(chars)) %>%
  layer_dropout(0.1)%>%
  layer_activation("softmax")
```

We require a *softmax* activation in the end, as we would like to interpret the final scores as probabilities; hence, it will be useful to have them between 0 and 1.

We now call the optimizer and compile our model:

```
optimizer <- optimizer_rmsprop(lr = 0.01)
model %>% compile(
  loss = "categorical_crossentropy",
  optimizer = optimizer
)
```

We have to specify a sampling function, which is a version of *softmax:*

```
sample_mod <- function(preds, temperature = 0.8){
  preds <- log(preds)/temperature
  exp_preds <- exp(preds)
  preds <- exp_preds/sum(exp(preds))
  rmultinom(1, 1, preds) %>%
  as.integer() %>%
  which.max()
}
```

Finally, we train our model:

```
history <- model %>% fit(
  X, y,
  batch_size = 128,
  epochs = 20
)
plot(history)
```

If everything went well, the history plot will show us a learning curve that looks like the following. This suggests that our model is training correctly:

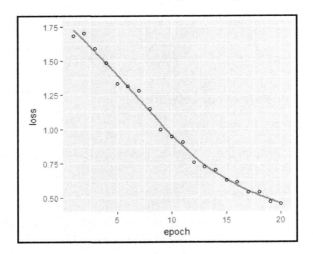

Training of our model in Keras

Perhaps we could increase the number of epochs? That's something you can try as an exercise!

It is now time to generate some of the samples:

```
start_idx <- sample(1:(length(text) - max_length), size = 1)
name <- text[start_idx:(start_idx + max_length - 1)]
generated <- ""
for(i in 1:10){
 x <- sapply(chars, function(x){
 as.integer(x == name)
 })
 dim(x) <- c(1, dim(x))
 preds <- predict(model, x)
 next_idx <- sample_mod(preds, 0.3)
 next_char <- chars[next_idx]

 generated <- str_c(generated, next_char, collapse = "")
 name <- c(name[-1], next_char)
 cat(generated)
 cat("\n\n")
}
```

With a simple modification of the preceding code you can generate names of different lengths. For this, we need to replace our preceding fixed length with a randomly sampled length, noted `random_len` in the following code snippet:

```
n_iter <- 100
for(iter in 1:n_iter){
   start_idx <- sample(1:(length(text) - max_length), size = 1)
   name <- text[start_idx:(start_idx + max_length - 1)]
   generated <- " "
   random_len <- sample(5:10,1)
   for(i in 1:random_len){
     x <- sapply(chars, function(x){
       as.integer(x == name)
     })
     dim(x) <- c(1, dim(x))
     preds <- predict(model, x)
     next_idx <- sample_mod(preds, 0.1)
     next_char <- chars[next_idx]
     generated <- str_c(generated, next_char)
     name <- c(name[-1], next_char)
     # cat(generated)
     # cat("\n\n")
   }
   cat(generated)
}
```

Among the generated samples (which might be different in your computer) are:

`Asarara, Laralaso`

Which sound rather convincingly like Spanish last names.

Of course, you can adapt the preceding model to any other text, perhaps including text like HTML or LaTeX.

A subtlety here is that we used character-level prediction. You can try to adapt the text to word-level prediction, to make it work like the auto-complete function of a smartphone.

Exercises

- Try the LSTM example for `Alice in Wonderland` to generate baby names using the datasets compiled by Mark Kantrowitz, available at: `https://www.cs.cmu.edu/Groups/AI/areas/nlp/corpora/names/0.html`.
- Music generation is also a sequential prediction problem, as we mentioned. You can take a look at the version of the Nottingham Music Database written in ABC notation at `http://abc.sourceforge.net/NMD/` to teach the computer to write music, using a similar recurrent neural network.
- Refactor the code on our recurrent neural network from scratch (the R6 implementation) so that it uses the `forward_step` function within the `bptt` function.
- We ignored bias terms in our recurrent neural network implementations. How will that affect the performance, if at all? Try to modify the code to include bias terms.
- Modify the code for the network using the cross-entropy method to use natural evolution strategies: `https://blog.openai.com/evolution-strategies/`.

Summary

In this chapter, we introduced different architectures for recurrent neural networks, and pointed out some of their limitations and capabilities. By introducing a naive Markovian model, we compared the efficiency of introducing such complicated architectures. When applied to the text generation problem, we saw that these different architectures had a noticeable improvement in the quality of the predictions. For training networks, we introduced different methods. The classical backpropagation algorithm and other gradient-free methods that are useful to solve black-box optimization problems.

5

Sentiment Analysis with Word Embeddings

In this chapter, we turn to the problem of sentiment analysis. Sentiment analysis is an umbrella term for a number of techniques to figure out how a speaker feels about a certain topic or piece of content.

A vanilla case study of sentiment analysis is **polarity**. Given a document or text string (for instance, a Tweet, a review, or a comment on a social network), the aim is to determine whether the author feels good, bad, or neutral about the item or topic in question.

At first look, this problem might seem trivial: A lookup table with positive and negative words, and simply counting the word frequencies should do, right? Not so fast. Here are a few examples of why this is tricky:

- Their decadent desserts made me hate myself
- You should try this place if you love cold food
- Disliking cake is not really my thing

What can we see in these examples?

- Negative terms used in a possibly positive sense
- Positive terms used sarcastically
- Two negative terms that imply something positive

 Note that we have not dealt with spelling mistakes, neologisms and use of multiple languages, just to name a few potential issues in real-life situations.

As you can see, sentiment analysis is a very complicated task, and we will merely scratch the surface.

The human element is the most important element in sentiment analysis. The accuracy of a sentiment analysis system depends on how much it agrees with human judgement. And how accurate could that be? Unfortunately not that much. Some researchers report disagreement rates as high as 20%. This means that if your sentiment analysis system has an accuracy of 70%, although seemingly unimpressive, it will still be good, since humans would agree on 80% of the classifications of a perfect sentiment analysis system. But, beware!

These figures are not exactly comparable, since the computer will have issues identifying subtleties that are best guessed by humans, such as sarcasm, jokes, or the subtle differences in meaning from the examples shown previously.

Nonetheless, there seems to be an increasing awareness from individuals and organizations about the importance of their presence online. We can measure that impact by the mushrooming of agencies and professionals specializing in social media monitoring. This has contributed to increased attention in the field from researchers (both in universities and industries), and we believe that it is likely that we will see significant advances in the area.

Our focus, as stated elsewhere in the book, is to introduce you to the algorithms in the simplest way possible. We will use a well-known dataset, which shares many of the properties of *real-life* datasets that you will find out there.

Warm-up – data exploration

Let's get things moving with a tiny example. Let's look at this tiny reviews corpus:

```
text <- c("The food is typical Czech, and the beer is good. The service is
quick, if short and blunt, and the waiting on staff could do with a bit of
customer service training",
        "The food was okay. Really not bad, but we had better",
        "A venue full of locals. No nonsense, no gimmicks. Only went for
drinks which were good and cheap. People friendly enough.",
        "Great food, lovely staff, very reasonable prices considering the
location!")
```

We will do some simple analysis here, which will help us appreciate some of the subtleties of sentiment analysis.

Working with tidy text

For this, we will use the `tidytext` package. This package is built on the philosophy of tidy data, introduced by Hadley Wickham in his 2014 paper (`https://www.jstatsoft.org/article/view/v059i10`). A dataset is tidy if the following three conditions are satisfied:

- Each variable is a column
- Each observation is a row
- Each type of observational unit is a table

The `tidytext` package helps us turn our text into tidy form, by putting one token per row. Let's start by loading `dplyr` and `tidytext`. If you don't have `tidytext`, install it first using `install.packages("tidytext")`.

Load the packages and let's transform our text into a data frame:

```
library(tidytext)
library(dplyr)
text_df <- data_frame(line = 1:4, text = text)
```

The `unnest_tokens` function is where the magic of `tidytext` begins:

```
text_df <- text_df %>%
 unnest_tokens(word, text)
head(text_df)
# A tibble: 6 x 2
    line word
   <int> <chr>
1 1 the
2 1 food
3 1 is
4 1 typical
5 1 czech
6 1 and
```

As you can see, our text was transformed as one token (the default is one word = one token) per row. First, let's get rid of stop words:

```
data(stop_words)
head(stop_words)
text_df <- text_df %>% anti_join(stop_words)
```

Our goal is to determine, at least visually by now, the sentiment of the preceding reviews. Let's begin with a quick summary of the word count:

```
library(ggplot2)
text_df %>%
  count(word, sort=T) %>%
  mutate(word = reorder(word, n)) %>%
  ggplot(aes(word, n)) +
  geom_col() +
  xlab(NULL) +
  coord_flip()+
  theme_bw()
```

We get a nice bar chart like this:

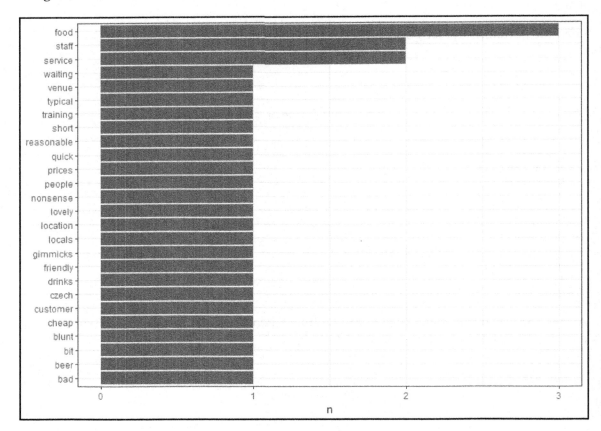

Basic word count in our toy review dataset

The `tidytext` package includes three lexicons (collection of words) annotated by sentiment:

- AFINN from Finn Årup Nielsen (http://www2.imm.dtu.dk/pubdb/views/publication_details.php?id=6010)
- bing from Bing Liu and collaborators (https://www.cs.uic.edu/~liub/FBS/sentiment-analysis.html)
- nrc from Saif Mohammad and Peter Turney (http://saifmohammad.com/WebPages/NRC-Emotion-Lexicon.htm)

The AFINN lexicon gives a numeric value between -5 and 5 to common words in English, with negative values being negative words. For instance:

```
get_sentiments("afinn") %>%
  filter(score==-5) %>%
  head
```

Gives (sensitive readers should skip the next snippet):

```
# A tibble: 6 x 2
        word score
       <chr> <int>
1 bastard    -5
2 bastards   -5
```

Whereas, the following:

```
get_sentiments("afinn") %>%
  filter(score==0) %>%
  head
```

Is simply:

```
# A tibble: 1 x 2
  word score
 <chr> <int>
1 some kind 0
```

And the following:

```
get_sentiments("afinn") %>%
  filter(score==5) %>%
  head
```

Returns:

```
# A tibble: 5 x 2
 word score
 <chr> <int>
1 breathtaking 5
2 hurrah 5
3 outstanding 5
4 superb 5
5 thrilled 5
```

The `bing` lexicon has only positive and negative words:

```
> get_sentiments("bing") %>% head
# A tibble: 6 x 2
 word sentiment
 <chr> <chr>
1 2-faced negative
2 2-faces negative
3 a+ positive
4 abnormal negative
5 abolish negative
6 abominable negative
```

Whereas, the `nrc` has different categories:

```
> get_sentiments("nrc") %>% head
# A tibble: 6 x 2
 word sentiment
 <chr> <chr>
1 abacus trust
2 abandon fear
3 abandon negative
4 abandon sadness
5 abandoned anger
6 abandoned fear
```

How can we use these word lists? Well, once our data is tidy, we can join them and create different aggregations to try to get a feeling of what is going on. Let's start by storing the `bing` lexicon somewhere:

```
bing <- get_sentiments("bing")
```

And joining it with our data:

```
> text_df %>% inner_join(bing) %>% count(line, sentiment)
Joining, by = "word"
# A tibble: 5 x 3
```

```
  line sentiment n
 <int> <chr> <int>
1 1 negative 1
2 2 negative 1
3 3 negative 3
4 3 positive 1
5 4 positive 2
```

Not bad, but we can always do better with a plot:

```
# Plot
text_df %>%
  inner_join(bing) %>%
  count(line,sentiment) %>%
  ggplot(aes(line, n, fill=sentiment))+
  geom_col()+
  coord_flip()+
  theme_bw()
```

The results are shown as follows. Not bad. We see that a simple join and a summary aggregation already gives a basic insight into how to classify the reviews by sentiment:

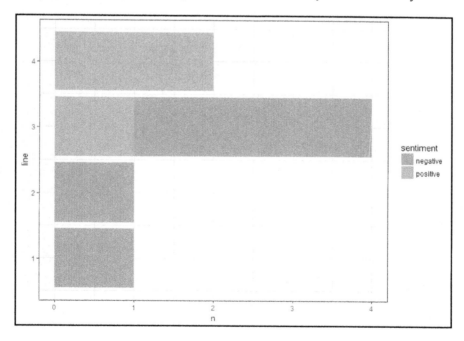

Aggregate statistics using the bing lexicon

This is already valuable, but in some cases we would like to know how positive or negative a review is; for instance, to redirect the issue to the proper customer service representative. In this case, it might be useful to use the AFINN lexicon instead:

```
afinn <- get_sentiments("afinn")
```

Now, we join the review data as before:

```
text_df %>% inner_join(afinn)
```

And look at the total score per review:

```
# Group
text_df %>%
  inner_join(afinn) %>%
  group_by(line) %>%
  summarize(total_score = sum(score))
```

Not bad; but again, it's better to make a plot:

```
# Plot
text_df %>%
  inner_join(afinn) %>%
  group_by(line) %>%
  summarize(total_score = sum(score)) %>%
  mutate(sentiment=ifelse(total_score>0,"positive","negative")) %>%
  ggplot(aes(line, total_score, fill=sentiment))+
  geom_col()+
  coord_flip()+
  theme_bw()
```

Which is shown here:

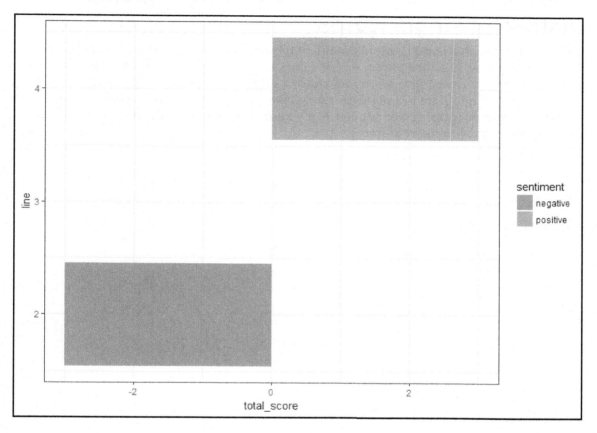

Aggregate statistics using the AFINN lexicon

Wow, what happened here? The situation looks a bit weird. First, note that one review has disappeared. This is because there are no common words with the AFINN lexicon for the first review (recall that we had an inner join). A bit more worrying is what has happened to the third review. The score is zero, which comes from summing the positive and negative scores of each word in the review, as per the AFINN lexicon. However, note that review 3 is mostly positive. What happened then?

The more, the merrier – calculating n-grams instead of single words

The reason for such an odd result in the previous section can be traced back to the context. Notice that review 3 had the phrase `No nonsense, no gimmicks`, which is largely positive, but has two negative words attached to it. How can we take context into account? Enter n-grams. An n-gram is a sequence of *n* consecutive items (words, or in the case of speech, phonemes) from a given sequence of text or speech. Let's make this clear with an example and use 2-grams, or bigrams:

```
text_df <- data_frame(line = 1:4, text = text)
text_df <- text_df %>%
  unnest_tokens(bigram, text, token="ngrams", n=2)
text_df
```

This gives us the following:

```
# A tibble: 70 x 2
  line bigram
  <int> <chr>
1 1 the food
2 1 food is
3 1 is typical
4 1 typical czech
5 1 czech and
6 1 and the
7 1 the beer
8 1 beer is
9 1 is good
10 1 good the
# ... with 60 more rows
```

So, we now see that consecutive words are put together. Already, this can be helpful enough to determine the negations of negative words that are actually positive, as in our preceding review 3. Let's find out which negative words are negated. First, we split the two words of the bigram into two columns:

```
library(tidyr)
text_df <- text_df %>% separate(bigram, c("w1","w2"), sep=" ")
text_df
```

Which gives us:

```
# A tibble: 70 x 3
  line w1 w2
 * <int> <chr> <chr>
 1 1 the food
 2 1 food is
 3 1 is typical
 4 1 typical czech
 5 1 czech and
 6 1 and the
 7 1 the beer
 8 1 beer is
 9 1 is good
10 1 good the
# ... with 60 more rows
```

A bit of `dplyr` magic brings the offending part of the sentence to question:

```
text_df %>%
  filter(w1=="no") %>%
  inner_join(afinn, by=c(w2="word"))
```

Which is:

```
# A tibble: 1 x 4
  line w1 w2 score
  <int> <chr> <chr> <int>
1 3 no nonsense -2
```

We could now use this information to override the score of our third review. However, note how involved a process it might be. Sure, in many cases it would work well, but we should find more systematic ways of dealing with context.

n-grams are important to keep track of the context of a word, and use it correctly for classification.

Bag of words benchmark

We came across one-hot embeddings while identifying fraudulent emails in Chapter 3, *Fraud Detection with Autoencoders*. The idea is to represent each word as a basis vector; that is, a vector with zeros except one coordinate. Hence, each document (a review in this case) is represented as a vector with ones and zeros. We went a bit further from that and used different weighting (tf-idf).

Let's revisit this model once again, but include n-grams instead of single words. This will be our benchmark for the more sophisticated word embeddings we will do later.

Preparing the data

The data is a subset of the Stanford Large Movie Review dataset, originally published in:

Andrew L. Maas, Raymond E. Daly, Peter T. Pham, Dan Huang, Andrew Y. Ng, and Christopher Potts. (2011). *Learning Word Vectors for Sentiment Analysis.* The 49th Annual Meeting of the Association for Computational Linguistics (ACL 2011).

This data is available to download at http://ai.stanford.edu/~amaas/data/sentiment/, provided proper credit is given to the original paper. This is the raw data, but you can find a preprocessed version in Kaggle, https://www.kaggle.com/c/word2vec-nlp-tutorial/data.

Let's begin with loading the data:

```
df <- read.csv("./data/labeledTrainData.tsv", encoding = "utf-8", quote =
"", sep="\t", stringsAsFactors = F)
text <- df$review
```

We revisit the tm library. Note that the code is a bit different, since we are loading the text as VCorpus instead of Corpus as before:

```
library(tm)
corpus <- VCorpus(VectorSource(text))
inspect(corpus[[1]])
```

Which yields the first review in this data:

```
> inspect(corpus[[1]])
<<PlainTextDocument>>
Metadata: 7
Content: chars: 1681

  stuff going moment mj ive started listening music watching odd documentary
watched wiz watched moonwalker maybe just want get certain insight guy
thought really cool eighties just maybe make mind whether guilty innocent
moonwalker part biography part feature film remember going see cinema
originally released subtle messages mjs feeling towards press also obvious
message drugs bad mkaybr br visually impressive course michael jackson
unless remotely like mj anyway going hate find boring may call mj egotist
consenting making movie mj fans say made fans true really nice himbr br
actual feature film bit finally starts 20 minutes excluding smooth criminal
sequence joe pesci convincing psychopathic powerful drug lord wants mj dead
bad beyond mj overheard plans nah joe pescis character ranted wanted people
know supplying drugs etc dunno maybe just hates mjs musicbr br lots ...
<truncated>
```

First, some preprocessing:

```
corpus <- tm_map(corpus,content_transformer(tolower))
corpus <- tm_map(corpus, content_transformer(removePunctuation))
corpus <- tm_map(corpus, content_transformer(removeWords),
stopwords("english"))
```

The next step is to create bigrams. We saw that this is important:

```
BigramTokenizer <- function(x){ unlist(lapply(ngrams(words(x), 2), paste,
collapse = " "), use.names = FALSE)}
dtm <- DocumentTermMatrix(corpus, control = list(tokenize =
BigramTokenizer))
dtm <- removeSparseTerms(dtm, 0.995)
X <- as.data.frame(as.matrix(dtm))
X$sentiment <- df$sentiment
X$sentiment <- ifelse(X$sentiment<0.5,0,1)
```

We are now ready to apply this data to a classification model; for instance, logistic regression.

Implementing a benchmark – logistic regression

Logistic regression might not be the fanciest algorithm in town, but for sure, it is one of the most commonly used. It is quite robust and powerful, yet simple to interpret. Unlike other methods, it is easy to look under the hood and see what it is doing.

First, we choose some indices for the training and testing set:

```
# Train, test, split
library(caTools)
set.seed(42)
spl <- sample.split(X$sentiment, 0.7)
train <- subset(X, spl == TRUE)
test <- subset(X, spl == FALSE)
```

And now we split into train and test sets:

```
X_train <- subset(train,select=-sentiment)
y_train <- train$sentiment
X_test <- subset(test,select=-sentiment)
y_test <- test$sentiment
```

Now let's look at the model and the coefficients:

```
model <- glm(y_train ~ ., data = X_train, family = "binomial")
coefs <- as.data.frame(model$coefficients)
names(coefs) <- c("value")
coefs$token <- row.names(coefs)
```

And see how the model is using each feature:

```
library(ggplot2)
library(dplyr)
coefs %>%
 arrange(desc(value)) %>%
 head %>%
 ggplot(aes(x=token, y=value))+
 geom_col()+
 coord_flip()+
 theme_bw()
```

This gives us the following chart:

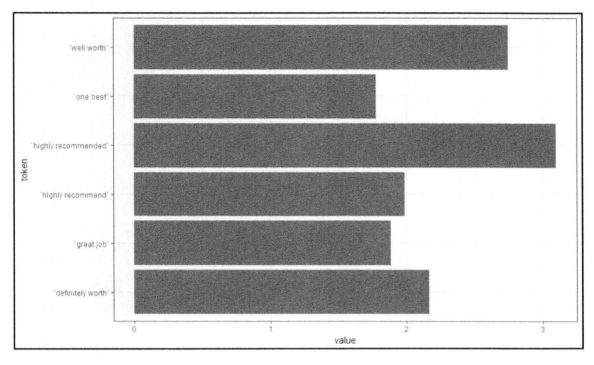

Features correlated with positive sentiment

Now let's take a look at the features correlated with a negative sentiment (try to do it yourself before looking at the code!):

```
coefs %>%
  arrange(value) %>%
  head %>%
  ggplot(aes(x=token, y=value))+
  geom_col()+
  coord_flip()+
  theme_bw()
```

This looks like:

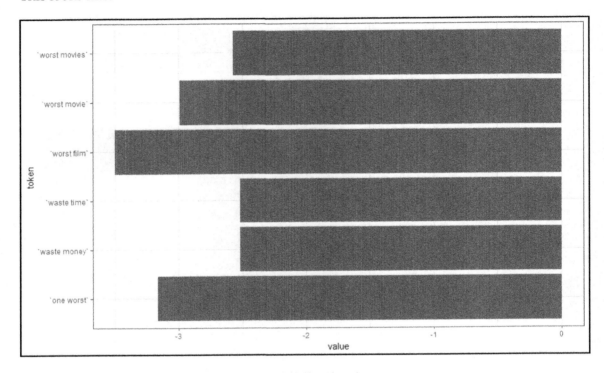

Features correlated with negative sentiment

Now let's take a closer look at the performance using the ROC curve. We can write our own function instead of using an extra package:

```
roc <- function(y_test, y_preds){
  y_test <- y_test[order(y_preds, decreasing = T)]
  return(data.frame(fpr=cumsum(!y_test)/sum(!y_test),
                    tpr=cumsum(y_test)/sum(y_test)) )
}
```

We can now generate predictions and plot the curve using the base R graphics:

```
y_preds <- predict(model, X_test, type="response")
plot(roc(y_test,y_preds), xlim=c(0,1), ylim=c(0,1))
```

Or store them on a data frame and use `ggplot2`:

```
roc_df <- roc(y_test,y_preds)
ggplot(roc_df, aes(x=fpr,y=tpr))+geom_point(color="red")+theme_bw()
```

The ROC curve looks like this:

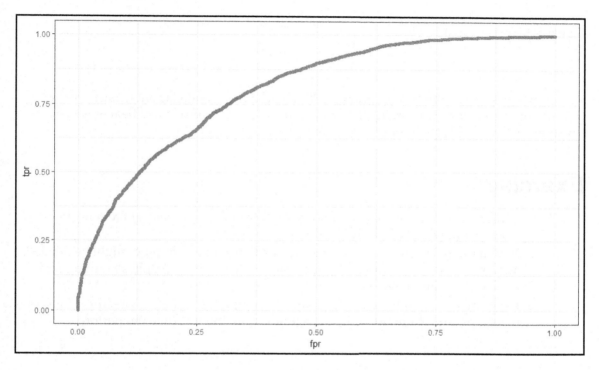

ROC curve for logistic regression with bigrams

We could quantify the AUC, but this is a bit more involved using base R code. You can try using the ROCR or pROC packages. We will simply set up a threshold of 0.5 and compute the precision for the positive class for that threshold, just to get a feel for what's going on:

```
labels <- ifelse(y_preds<0.5,0,1)
table(labels,y_test)
```

This gives:

```
table(labels,y_test)
 y_test
labels    0     1
  0     2536  896
  1     1214 2854
```

So we get a precision of:

```
2536/(2536+896)
[1] 0.7389277
```

For the positive class. Not bad, in practice; 80% would be a good classifier, since this is roughly the agreement rate among humans. You can try to improve this benchmark in a few different ways, suggested in the *Exercises* section.

Exercises

1. Explore the performance of your classifier for different values of *n* in n-grams. Does it change significantly?
2. The charts in the previous section suggest that some stemming might be needed, as some of the top features are quite similar in meaning. Apply stemming and look at the shape of the ROC curve.
3. Experiment with other classifiers, for instance, random forests or support vector machines, and different kinds of n-grams. Can you improve the performance?

Word embeddings

The field of **natural language processing (NLP)** is advancing pretty quickly these days, as much as modern data science and artificial intelligence.

Algorithms such as word2vec (Mikolov and others, 2013) and GloVe (Pennington and others, 2014) have been pioneers in the field, and although strictly neither of them is related to deep learning, the models trained with them are used as input data in many applications of deep learning to NLP.

We will briefly describe word2vec and GloVe, which are perhaps the most commonly used algorithms for word embedding, although research in the intersection of neural networks and language goes back to at least Jeff Elman in the 1990s.

word2vec

The word2vec algorithm (or, rather, family of algorithms) takes a text corpus as input and produces the word vectors as output. It first constructs a vocabulary from the training text data and then learns vector representation of words. Then we use those vectors as features for machine learning algorithms.

Word vectors are able to catch some intuitive regularities in the language, for instance:

vector('Paris') - vector('France') + vector('Italy')

Results in a vector that is very close to:

vector('Rome'),

And,

vector('king') - vector('man') + vector('woman')

Is close to:

vector('queen').

What does word2vec do behind the scenes? word2vec arrives at word vectors by training a neural network to predict:

- A word in the center from its surroundings (continuous bag of words, CBOW)
- A word's surroundings from the center word (skip-gram model)

Why is that useful? According to the distributional hypothesis, words occurring together tend to convey similar meanings. Researchers Goldberg and Levy point out (https://arxiv.org/abs/1402.3722) that the word2vec objective function causes words that occur in similar contexts to have similar embeddings, which is in line with the distributional hypothesis. However, they also point out that a better explanation is required.

> The distributional hypothesis states that words that are used in the same contexts are related. This is an underlying assumption of vector embedding algorithms such as GloVe or word2vec.

GloVe

About a year after word2vec, researchers at Stanford published a paper (http://web.stanford.edu/~jpennin/papers/glove.pdf) that explicitly identifies the objective that word2vec optimizes under the hood. Their method, **GloVe**, (**global vectors**) explicitly names the objective matrix, identifies the factorization, and provides some intuitive justification as to why this should give us working similarities.

 This section describes, at a high level, the inner workings of the GloVe algorithm. As such, it is a bit more math-heavy than we would have wanted. If you are not familiar with linear algebra and calculus, you can safely skip it.

How does GloVe work?

1. Create a word **co-occurrence matrix** where each entry represents how often word *i* appears in the context of word *j*. This matrix is clearly symmetric. Moreover, for each term, we look for words co-occurring on certain windows, and give less weight to more distant words.
2. Define soft constraints for each word pair.
3. Finally, introduce a cost function that penalizes learning from very common word pairs.
   For the soft constraints, we mean:

$$w_i^T w_j + b_i + b_j = log(X_{ij})$$

Where the w_i and w_j denote the main and context embedded vectors, respectively, with biases b_i and b_j, and X_{ij} is the co-occurrence of word *j* in the context of word *i*.

The cost function is defined by:

$$\sum_{i,j}^{V} f(X_{i,j}).(w_i^T w_j - b_i - b_j - log(Xij))^2$$

Where *V* is the vocabulary and *f* is defined by:

$$f(X_{ij}) = \begin{cases} (\frac{X_{ij}}{X_{max}})^\alpha & , \quad X_{ij} < X_{max} \\ 1 & , \quad X_{ij} \geq X_{max} \end{cases}$$

Where *alpha* and X_{max} are hyperparameters that you can choose.

Sentiment analysis from movie reviews

Let's continue with the IMDb data and put into practice the ideas from the previous sections. In this section, we will use a few familiar packages, like `tidytext`, `plyr` and `dplyr`, as well as the excellent `text2vec` by Dimitriy Selivanov, which was released in 2017, and the well-known `caret` package by Max Kuhn.

Data preprocessing

We need to prepare our data for the algorithm.

First, a few imports that will be necessary:

```
library(plyr)
library(dplyr)
library(text2vec)
library(tidytext)
library(caret)
```

We will use the IMDb data as before:

```
imdb <- read.csv("./data/labeledTrainData.tsv", encoding = "utf-8", quote =
"", sep="\t", stringsAsFactors = F)
```

And create an iterator over the tokens:

```
tokens <- space_tokenizer(imdb$review)
token_iterator <- itoken(tokens)
```

The tokens are simple words, also known as **unigrams**. This constitutes our vocabulary:

```
vocab <- create_vocabulary(token_iterator)
```

It's important for the co-occurrence matrix to include only words that appear frequently together a significant amount of times. We will set this threshold to 5 :

```
vocab <- prune_vocabulary(vocab, term_count_min = 5)
```

We use our filtered vocabulary:

```
vectorizer <- vocab_vectorizer(vocab)
```

And set up a window of size 5 for context words:

```
tcm <- create_tcm(token_iterator, vectorizer, skip_grams_window = 5)
```

Now that we have the co-occurrence matrix, let's continue with the vector embedding.

From words to vectors

We are ready to create the word embedding using GloVe. First, let's initialize an instance of the GlobalVectors class:

```
glove <- GlobalVectors$new(word_vectors_size = 50,
                           vocabulary = vocab,
                           x_max = 10)
```

We now apply the `fit_transform` method (scikit learn users might be familiar with it):

```
wv_main <- glove$fit_transform(tcm,
                               n_iter = 10,
                               convergence_tol = 0.01)
```

And once this is done, we have our vectorizer ready. We now need to parse our text:

```
text <- unlist(imdb$review)
length(text)
# 25000
text_df <- data_frame(line = 1:25000, text = text)
```

And apply the `unnest_tokens` functions from `tidytext` to turn our data in a tidy format:

```
text_df <- text_df %>%
  unnest_tokens(word, text)
head(text_df)
```

This gives a familiar output:

```
  head(text_df)
# A tibble: 6 x 2
  line word
  <int> <chr>
1 1 with
2 1 all
3 1 this
4 1 stuff
5 1 going
6 1 down
```

But wait, what about the GloVe? Let's take a look:

```
head(wv_main[,1:3])
             [,1]  [,2]  [,3]
overpowered 0.03408282 -0.225022092 0.077734992
nears 0.65971708 -0.005281781 -0.100175403
producers) 0.46528772 0.063937798 -0.165794402
Daddy, 0.06035958 -0.076200403 0.008196513
rhetoric, -0.05500082 0.149410397 -0.314875215
Johnsons' 0.43385875 0.078220785 -0.177165091
```

Actually the `text2vec` package returns two objects:

```
wv_context <- glove$components
```

We can use either `wv_main` or `wv_context` as our vector embedding, but it sometimes helps (according to the GloVe paper) to put them together. So, you can create a `wv` object as the sum or average of these two vectors, for instance:

```
wv <- wv_main + t(wv_context).
```

Let's use only the `wv_main` for now. We need to coerce the matrix to a data frame format and add `row.names` as a column, to join it with our text, in tidy format:

```
wv <- as.data.frame(wv_main)
wv$word <- row.names(wv)
```

And finally, put these two together:

```
df <-  wv%>% inner_join(text_df)
```

This is still not ready to use as we need to aggregate the vectors as they appear in the review. One possibility is to just take the average vector as representative; the vector of the review would be the average vector of all the words that compose the review. We will take this approach here and suggest some other possibilities in the exercises:

```
df <- df %>%
        group_by(line) %>%
        summarize_all(mean) %>%
        select(1:50)
df$label <- as.factor(imdb$sentiment)
```

This data is now ready for passing through different classifiers, from which we can predict the sentiment polarity (positive/negative).

Sentiment extraction

We will use `caret` to try different classifiers at once:

```
library(caret)
```

We first need to prepare the training scheme:

```
control <- trainControl(method="cv", repeats=5)
```

And we will set up the different models to try:

- Random forest
- Gradient boosting machines
- Logit boost
- Naive Bayes

Do not forget to set the seed for the random number generator, to make the results repeatable:

```
set.seed(7)
 modelRF <- train(
                    label~.,
                    data=df,
                    method="rf",
                    trControl=control
                  )

    modelGbm <- train(
                    label~.,
                    data=df,
                    method="gbm",
                    trControl=control,
                    verbose=FALSE
                  )

modelLogitBoost <- train(
                    label~.,
                    data=df,
                    method="LogitBoost",
                    trControl=control
```

```
                           )

modelNaiveBayes <- train(
                       label~.,
                       data=df,
                       method="nb",
                       trControl=control
                       )
```

The training will take some time, but once this is done, we can collect the results in a data frame for later exploration:

```
results <- resamples(
                   list(
                       RF=modelRF,
                       GBM=modelGbm,
                       LB=modelLogitBoost,
                       NB=modelNaiveBayes
                       )
                   )
```

We can easily get a summary of the results, with the familiar summary function:

```
> summary(results)

Call:
summary.resamples(object = results)

Models: RF, GBM, LB, NB
Number of resamples: 10

Accuracy
      Min. 1st Qu. Median Mean 3rd Qu. Max. NA's
RF 0.7116 0.7189 0.7284 0.72732 0.7363 0.7412 0
GBM 0.7168 0.7199 0.7352 0.73228 0.7410 0.7496 0
LB 0.5680 0.5933 0.6124 0.60656 0.6184 0.6420 0
NB 0.6244 0.6291 0.6374 0.63992 0.6510 0.6588 0

Kappa
      Min. 1st Qu. Median Mean 3rd Qu. Max. NA's
RF 0.4232 0.4378 0.4568 0.45464 0.4726 0.4824 0
GBM 0.4336 0.4398 0.4704 0.46456 0.4820 0.4992 0
LB 0.1360 0.1866 0.2248 0.21312 0.2368 0.2840 0
NB 0.2488 0.2582 0.2748 0.27984 0.3020 0.3176 0
```

Or more detailed visualizations with:

```
bwplot(results)
```

The preceding code produces the following metrics:

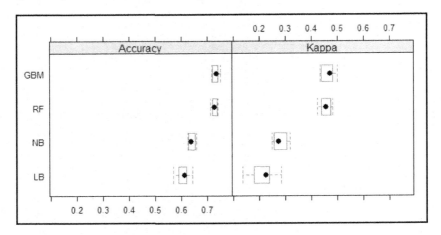

Boxplot comparing the performance of different classifiers on top of GloVe

You can also do it with:

```
dotplot(results)
```

Anyhow, time to look at the performance metrics!

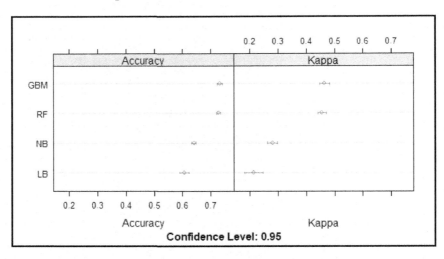

Dotplot comparing the performance of different classifiers on top of GloVe

On the plots and the preceding summary results shown, the **accuracy** is the percentage of correctly classified instances out of all instances, whereas the **kappa** metric (or Cohen's kappa statistic) is the accuracy normalized with the baseline random classification for your data, as if every observation were classified according to the probability distribution given by the frequency of each class.

 A kappa of zero means that the model is useless (kappa is between 0 and 1) and the higher the kappa, the more likely your model is useful, although there is no unified interpretation of this statistic.

So we see that tree-based methods tend to do quite well. This is somehow in contrast to one-hot encoding models. It is usually not recommended to use tree-based methods in data with a large number of sparse features, which would be the case if we had one-hot encoded models as before. Since we are instead embedding into dense vectors, trees are welcome again and they do perform well, even without tweaking hyperparameters.

The importance of data cleansing

If you follow the preceding workflow, and stop from time to time to see the results (which you absolutely should, by the way) you will notice that there is a lot of garbage around—words with upper and lower case, punctuation and so on. What happens if you improve this workflow by properly parsing the words? You can use the tokenizers library instead of the `space_tokenizer` function from text2vec to remove stopwords and punctuation in a single line:

```
library(tokenizers)
tokens <- tokenize_words(imdb$review, stopwords = stopwords())
```

The full code is now:

```
library(plyr)
library(dplyr)
library(text2vec)
library(tidytext)
library(caret)

imdb <- read.csv("./data/labeledTrainData.tsv"
                , encoding = "utf-8"
                , quote = ""
                , sep="\t"
                , stringsAsFactors = F)
# Standard preprocessing: change to lowercase, remove english stopwords and
```

```
punctuation
library(tokenizers)
tokens <- tokenize_words(imdb$review, stopwords = stopwords())


# Create vocabulary. The tokens are simple words here.
token_iterator <- itoken(tokens)
vocab <- create_vocabulary(token_iterator)

# Kill sparse terms
vocab <- prune_vocabulary(vocab, term_count_min = 5L)

vectorizer <- vocab_vectorizer(vocab)

# use window of 5 for context words
 tcm <- create_tcm(token_iterator, vectorizer, skip_grams_window = 5L)

glove <- GlobalVectors$new(word_vectors_size = 50,
                         vocabulary = vocab,
                         x_max = 10)
wv_main <- glove$fit_transform(tcm,
                             n_iter = 10,
                             convergence_tol = 0.05)

text <- unlist(imdb$review)

text_df <- data_frame(line = 1:25000, text = text)

text_df <- text_df %>%
        unnest_tokens(word, text)

wv <- as.data.frame(wv_main)

wv$word <- row.names(wv)

df <- wv%>% inner_join(text_df)

# Now we need to create the trained matrix
df <- df %>% group_by(line) %>% summarize_all(mean) %>% select(1:51)
df$label <- as.factor(imdb$sentiment)

library(caret)

control <- trainControl(method="cv", repeats=5)


# Train the different models
set.seed(7)
```

```
modelRF <- train(label~., data=df, method="rf", trControl=control)

set.seed(7)
modelGbm <- train(label~., data=df, method="gbm", trControl=control,
verbose=FALSE)

set.seed(7)
modelLogitBoost <- train(label~., data=df, method="LogitBoost",
trControl=control)

set.seed(7)
modelNaiveBayes <- train(label~., data=df, method="nb", trControl=control)
```

```
# collect resamples: this is useful for the plots
results <- resamples(
                    list(RF=modelRF,
                    GBM=modelGbm,
                    LB=modelLogitBoost,
                    NB=modelNaiveBayes))
```

```
# summarize and check the model performance
summary(results)
bwplot(results)
dotplot(results)
```

We can see a significant improvement in the results!

```
> summary(results)
Call:
summary.resamples(object = results)
Models: RF, GBM, LB, NB
Number of resamples: 10
Accuracy
 Min. 1st Qu. Median Mean 3rd Qu. Max. NA's
RF 0.7820 0.7892 0.7946 0.79340 0.7972 0.8012 0
GBM 0.7904 0.7952 0.7978 0.79732 0.7996 0.8036 0
LB 0.6904 0.6978 0.7040 0.70388 0.7098 0.7176 0
NB 0.6728 0.6810 0.6900 0.68824 0.6957 0.7008 0
```

The dotplot and boxplot here are shown as follows:

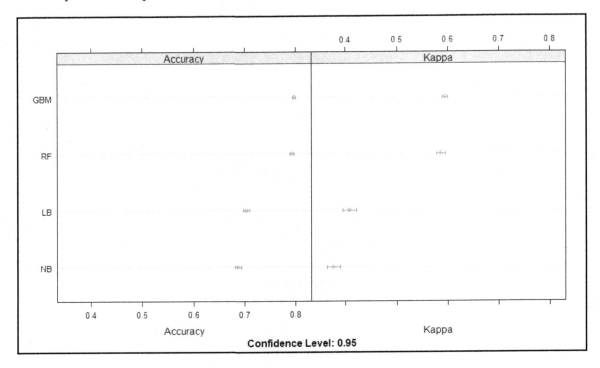

Dotplot showing the different classifiers after proper preprocessing

And the boxplot:

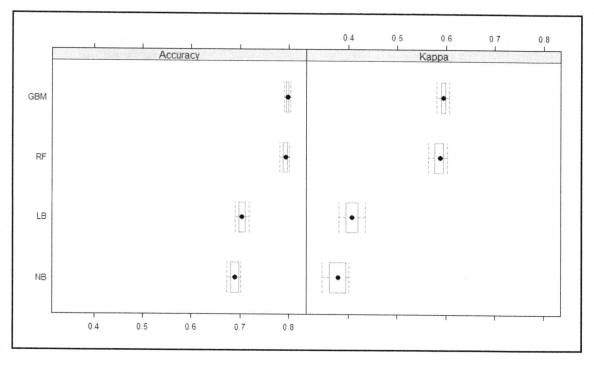

Boxplot showing the different classifiers after proper preprocessing

Remember, when it comes to software in general, and data science is not the exception:

 Garbage in, garbage out: Always pay attention to the data you are feeding to the models! The most powerful models available will produce unsatisfactory results when feeding them with the wrong data! It's important to log, or at least print, to the console, any preprocessing steps you are doing. Treating models as a magic black box is a very dangerous thing, and unfortunately too common.

As we mentioned earlier, vector embeddings is not proper deep learning, rather a feature representation method. However, we can combine vector embeddings with deep neural networks and, hopefully, get better results.

Vector embeddings and neural networks

It's time to combine vector embeddings and neural networks to, hopefully, create more robust models. Let's do a simple extension to our workflow by training a neural network as a classifier. We start with the now familiar preprocessing and vector embedding:

```
library(plyr)
library(dplyr)
library(text2vec)
library(tidytext)
library(caret)
library(tokenizers)

imdb <- read.csv("./data/labeledTrainData.tsv"
                , encoding = "utf-8"
                , quote = ""
                , sep="\t"
                , stringsAsFactors = F)

tokens <- tokenize_words(imdb$review, stopwords = stopwords())

# Boring boilerplate preprocessing
token_iterator <- itoken(tokens)
vocab <- create_vocabulary(token_iterator)
vocab <- prune_vocabulary(vocab, term_count_min = 5L)
vectorizer <- vocab_vectorizer(vocab)

# Create context and embedding
tcm <- create_tcm(token_iterator, vectorizer, skip_grams_window = 5L)
glove <- GlobalVectors$new(word_vectors_size = 50,
 vocabulary = vocab,
 x_max = 10)
wv_main = glove$fit_transform(tcm,
 n_iter = 10,
 convergence_tol = 0.01)
text <- unlist(imdb$review)
text_df <- data_frame(line = 1:length(text), text = text)
text_df <- text_df %>%
 unnest_tokens(word, text)
```

Let's try now with the context vector as well, instead of the main word vector:

```
wv_context <- glove$components
wv <- as.data.frame(wv_main+t(wv_context))
wv$word <- row.names(wv)
df <- wv%>% inner_join(text_df)
```

To then finally create the trained matrix:

```
df <- df %>% group_by(line) %>% summarize_all(mean) %>% select(1:51)
df$label <- as.factor(imdb$sentiment)
```

And finally, create a baseline neural network model with a single layer:

```
library(keras)

X <- df[,2:51]
y <- df[,52]

y <- to_categorical(y[["label"]])
y <- y[,2:3]

model <- keras_model_sequential()
model %>%
  layer_dense(activation='relu', units =20, input_shape=c(50))%>%
  layer_dense(units=2, activation = 'softmax')

model %>% compile(
  loss = 'categorical_crossentropy',
  optimizer = optimizer_rmsprop(),
  metrics = c('accuracy')
  )

history <- model %>% keras::fit(
  as.matrix(X), y,
  epochs = 30, batch_size = 128,
  validation_split = 0.2
  )
```

Calling the fit method triggers the training procedure. Once the training is done, we can see how it went by using the `plot` function:

```
plot(history)
```

Which gives us some slightly disappointing results:

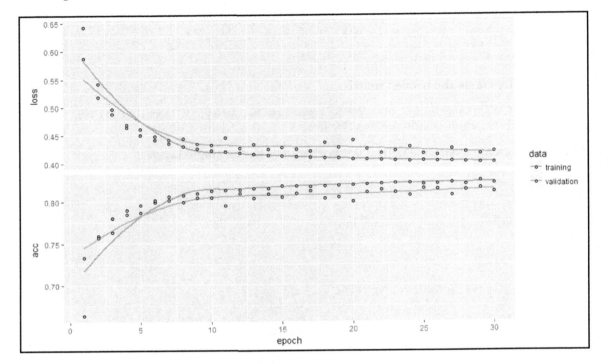

Performance of our single layer neural network with 20 neurons

Why is that disappointing? Well, our mighty neural network with 20 neurons did not improve upon, say, random forests. How can we improve this result?

It seems to be that neural networks in this case, or at least feed-forward neural networks might not be of much help here, or at least we were not able to find significant improvements by adding more layers. Actually it seemed to worsen results with three or more layers, and we even observed over-fitting.

 Occam's razor should prevail. The model you keep should be as simple as possible. A complicated model might be of little use in production because of the technical complications needed to deploy it. Furthermore, when we have no way of interpreting the model, unexpected results might happen when the model is applied to slightly different data from that used for training and testing.

We can save both our vector embedding and model for later use:

```
write.csv(wv,"./data/wv.csv", row.names = F)
save_model_hdf5(model, "glove_nn.hdf5")
```

Bi-directional LSTM networks

Well, our model did not quite work before with simple feed-forward networks. In this section, we will try a different model: Bi-directional LSTM networks.

Recall that LSTM networks preserve parts of the previous information via the hidden state. However, this information is only about the **past**.

Bidirectional LSTM run both ways—from past to future and back! The LSTM that runs backwards preserves information from the **future**. Using the two hidden states combined, you are able to keep the context of both past and future. Clearly this would not make sense for stock price prediction! Their use was initially justified in the domain of speech recognition because, as you might know from experience, the context of the full phrase is often needed to understand the meaning of a word. This happens, for instance, when you are trying to simultaneously translate from one language to another.

Ok, so how do we do this? Let's come back to `keras`. This will make the experience rather smooth, as we have seen before.

For the bidirectional LSTM API, keras expects, per row, one document with a list of words, which are passed over sequentially.

Let's begin with some familiar preprocessing steps:

```
library(purrr)
library(stringr)
library(tm)
library(keras)

df <- read.csv("./data/labeledTrainData.tsv", encoding = "utf-8", quote =
"", sep="\t", stringsAsFactors = F)

text <- df$review

corpus <- VCorpus(VectorSource(text))
corpus <- tm_map(corpus, content_transformer(tolower))
corpus <- tm_map(corpus, content_transformer(removePunctuation))
corpus <- tm_map(corpus, content_transformer(removeNumbers))
corpus <- tm_map(corpus, content_transformer(removeWords),
```

```
stopwords("english"))
dtm <- DocumentTermMatrix(corpus)
dtm <- removeSparseTerms(dtm, sparse=0.99)

X <- as.data.frame(as.matrix(dtm))
```

This returns a huge document-term matrix that has a lot of zeros. Now, we need to parse it to keep only the indices of the words that have non-zero values:

```
vocab <- names(X)
maxlen <- 100
dataset <- map(
 1:nrow(X),
 ~list(review = which(X[.x,]!=0))
)
dataset <- transpose(dataset)
```

And finally vectorize this in a usable way:

```
X <- array(0, dim = c(length(dataset$review), maxlen))
y <- array(0, dim = c(length(dataset$review)))
for(i in 1:length(dataset$review)){
  for(j in 1:maxlen){
    if(length(dataset$review[[i]])>j){
      X[i,j] <- dataset$review[[i]][j]
    }
    else{
      X[i,j] <- 0
    }
  }
  y[i] <- df[i,"sentiment"]
}

X <- as.matrix(X)
```

Which gives us:

```
> X[1,]
 [1] 23 46 49 65 71 100 109 115 137 144 149 161 165 185 188 190 193 196 210
217 235 271
[23] 286 287 295 308 317 326 359 365 366 376 380 390 407 436 441 464 469
483 494 498 511 514
[45] 520 521 571 580 585 588 595 603 613 628 662 693 705 726 734 742 749
760 776 795 797 803
[67] 808 828 832 843 848 852 871 872 890 892 897 900 908 922 929 931 955
973 975 983 994 1008
[89] 1019 1044 1072 1127 1140 1144 1184 1205 1217 1315 1317 1321
```

On each row, we have the first 100 words of the review, and we added zeros to the end if the review was shorter than 100 words. Now, we are ready to define our network:

```
# Initialize model
model <- keras_model_sequential()
model %>%
  # Creates dense embedding layer; outputs 3D tensor
  # with shape (batch_size, sequence_length, output_dim)
            layer_embedding(input_dim = length(vocab),
            output_dim = 128,
            input_length = maxlen) %>%
  bidirectional(layer_lstm(units = 64)) %>%
  layer_dropout(rate = 0.5) %>%
  layer_dense(units = 1, activation = 'sigmoid')
```

A few comments are in order here: First, note that the output layer is one-dimensional instead of two-dimensional, as before. This is purely for pedagogic purposes, and in the multi-class setup you would prefer to use similar code as before. Next, observe that there is a `layer_embedding` function, which is used for passing sequential data. Finally, the layer corresponding to the bidirectional LSTM comes, followed by a dropout.

Wait, what is dropout? **Dropout** is a technique introduced recently that simply *forgets* to train some neurons. This might seem weird, but in reality it is a very efficient way of performing model averaging with neural networks. In a similar way that averaging trees produces better models (less prone to over-fitting), averaging weaker neural networks results in a more robust model.

Now, we compile the model (note the different loss function, due to the different output):

```
# Compile: you can try different compilers
model %>% compile(
  loss = 'binary_crossentropy',
  optimizer = 'adam',
  metrics = c('accuracy')
)
```

And we are now ready to call the `fit` method:

```
> history <- model %>% fit(
  X, y,
  batch_size = 128,
  epochs = 4,
  validation_size = 0.2
  )
Epoch 1/4
25000/25000 [==============================] - 155s - loss: 0.4428 - acc:
```

```
0.7886
Epoch 2/4
25000/25000 [==============================] - 161s - loss: 0.3162 - acc:
0.8714
Epoch 3/4
25000/25000 [==============================] - 166s - loss: 0.2983 - acc:
0.8770
Epoch 4/4
25000/25000 [==============================] - 176s - loss: 0.2855 - acc:
0.8825

# Train model over four epochs
history <- model %>% fit(
  X, y,
  batch_size = 128,
  epochs = 4,
  validation_size = 0.2
)

> plot(history)
```

Not bad, we reach very good accuracy with LSTMs, significantly above feed-forward networks.

Other LSTM architectures

Bidirectional LSTM seemed to be a good idea, right? What about a simpler network architecture?

Instead of a bidirectional LSTM, we can consider a simple LSTM. To do this, we can replace the preceding model (after doing the same preprocessing; that is, feeding the data in the same format) with a simple LSTM:

```
model <- keras_model_sequential()
model %>%
 layer_embedding(input_dim = length(vocab),
 output_dim = 128,
 input_length = 100) %>%
 layer_lstm(units = 64, dropout = 0.2, recurrent_dropout = 0.2) %>%
 layer_dense(units = 1, activation = 'sigmoid')

model %>% compile(
    loss = "binary_crossentropy",
    optimizer = "adam",
```

```
    metrics = "accuracy"
)
```

After training, we get the following results:

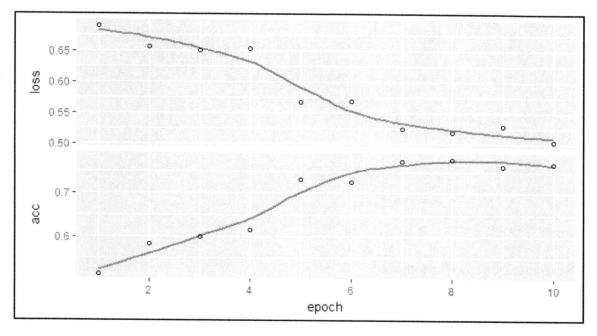

Training an LSTM in the IMDb data

So, as you can see, we experienced a significant loss in quality. This dataset is unfortunately too small for vanilla LSTMs to beat simpler configurations, such as tf-idf and logistic regression, or our GloVe + random forest experiment.

Notice also the different shape of the loss. An interesting, if not completely clear (at least to us), issue that calls our attention is the difference in shape—a small bump instead of exponential decay. This is not unusual to see in LSTMs, as opposed to other architectures, such as feed-forward networks or convolutional neural networks.

Actually, now that we mention CNNs, they can be used in language, too!:

```
# Initialize model
model <- keras_model_sequential()

model %>%
  layer_embedding(
```

```
                       input_dim = length(vocab),
                       output_dim = 128,
                       input_length = 100
                        ) %>%
   layer_dropout(0.25) %>%
   layer_conv_1d(
                   filters=64,
                   kernel_size=5,
                   padding = "valid",
                   activation = "relu",
                   strides = 1
             )  %>%
   layer_max_pooling_1d(pool_size=4)  %>%
   layer_lstm(70) %>%
   layer_dense(1) %>%
   layer_activation("sigmoid")

model %>% compile(
 loss = "binary_crossentropy",
 optimizer = "adam",
 metrics = "accuracy"
)
```

The results are shown as follows:

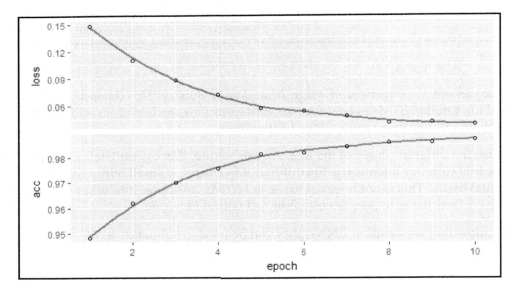

Results for a combination of a CNN and an LSTM network

We get an almost too impressive performance. How do CNNs work in text? In a similar way as they work in pictures, one-dimensional convolutional neural networks are convolved with the input layer over a spatial window length (five in our example). It is certainly easier to imagine *average of colors/intensity* on a certain window in an image, and we would not like to push an analogy that makes no sense. As the field is evolving so fast, perhaps soon we would have a more satisfactory explanation of the effectiveness of CNN in sentiment analysis tasks. For the time being, let's be glad that they work fine and can be trained reasonably fast.

 Beware that, for the sake of brevity, in most of the examples in this chapter we have omitted the verification of the results on the validation set (which is still the right thing to do, even if we rely on Keras' validation mechanism). So do not take the scores presented at face value.

Exercises

- Use the *context vector*, or a combination of the context vector and the main vector from GloVe. How do the results change? You can also build a meta-model that calculates the appropriate weight you should give to each vector.
- Do the results improve significantly if we use stemming?
- Can you improve the results by playing with the parameters of GloVe? You can tweak `skip_grams_window` for instance, or the number of iterations.
- You can also try to implement `fastText` (`https://keras.rstudio.com/articles/examples/imdb_fasttext.html`) using `keras`.

Mining sentiment from Twitter

It's time to put our knowledge of different sentiment classification models in a more realistic scenario—Twitter sentiment analysis.

As we mentioned in the introduction, sentiment analysis is of great interest for all companies that have a presence online (which is, well, lots of companies in many countries). It is also relevant for politicians, researchers, stock traders and others.

Before using any service or API, be sure to review their *terms of service* and follow them! We do not encourage unlawful behavior in any way.

Connecting to the Twitter API

Luckily for us, there is a nice package in R to retrieve our Tweets: The library `twitteR`. First, there are a number of steps you need to follow:

1. If you do not have one, create a Twitter account to be able to access their API.
2. Go to `https://dev.twitter.com/apps` and log in with your credentials.
3. Once logged in, click on **Create New App**.
4. Put this as callback URL `http://localhost:1410`.
5. Now go to **Keys and Access Tokens** and then **Create my access token**.
6. You should have a screen showing you four things:
   - **Consumer key**
   - **Consumer secret**
   - **Access token**
   - **Access secret**

Use them in the following snippet to gather some Tweets:

```
#install.packages("twitteR")
library(twitteR)

# Change the next four lines based on your own consumer_key,
consume_secret, access_token, and access_secret.
consumer_key <- "YOUR CONSUMER KEY"
consumer_secret <- "YOUR CONSUMER SECRET"
access_token <- "YOUR ACCESS TOKEN"
access_secret <- "YOUR ACCESS SECRET"

setup_twitter_oauth(consumer_key, consumer_secret, access_token,
access_secret)
tw = twitteR::searchTwitter('#something'
                            , n = 1e4
                            , since = '2017-12-08'
                            , retryOnRateLimit = 1e3)
d = twitteR::twListToDF(tw)
```

Note that this is merely for demonstration purposes, but remember, you should use the APIs responsibly and at your own risk and responsibility.

Building our model

If you have a Twitter account and you would like to analyze your own history, you can follow the official instructions on their website (https://help.twitter.com/en/managing-your-account/how-to-download-your-twitter-archive) and you will receive a ZIP file with your own Tweet history.

We will use Pablo's Twitter data for demonstration.

Exploratory data analysis

As explained earlier in this chapter, one thing you can do is to look for an annotated lexicon per sentiment and try to do some basic analysis there, thanks to the package tidytext.

First, we import a few libraries that would come handy and load our Twitter history:

```
library(plyr)
library(dplyr)
library(tidytext)
library(ggplot2)
df <- read.csv("./data/Tweets.csv", stringsAsFactors = F)
text_df <- data_frame(tweet_id=df$tweet_id, tweet=df$text)
```

Now, we use the unnest_tokens function to bring the data into tidy format:

```
text_df <- text_df %>%
  unnest_tokens(word, tweet)
```

And remove the stop words:

```
data(stop_words)
head(stop_words)
text_df <- text_df %>% anti_join(stop_words)
```

Once this is done, we join it with, for instance, the bing lexicon:

```
bing <- get_sentiments("bing")
text_df %>% inner_join(bing)
```

And we are ready!

```
# Plot
text_df %>%
  inner_join(bing) %>%
  count(sentiment) %>%
  ggplot(aes(sentiment, n, fill=sentiment))+
  geom_col()+
  theme_bw()
```

What do we learn from this? Well, that Pablo is a bit more of a negative person on Twitter, as the data shows. Unfortunately, it is our duty as data scientists to present the facts, even when they are not favorable to us.

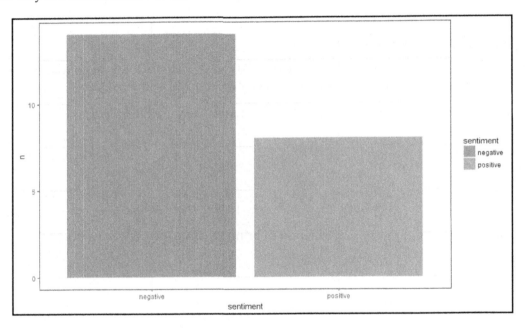

Pablo is slightly more negative in Twitter than in person

Using a trained model

Alternatively, and perhaps more interestingly, we can use a trained model to predict sentiment. We can train our model in a larger corpus and then simply apply it online to the new examples that come.

First, let's load our model and the vector embedding that we trained before for the movie reviews:

```
wv <- read.csv("./data/wv.csv")
model <- load_model_hdf5("glove_nn.hdf5")
```

As before, we join the vector representations with the data in tidy form:

```
df <- wv%>% inner_join(text_df)
```

And take the average of those vectors per Tweet as the embedded representation of our Tweet:

```
df <- df %>% group_by(tweet_id) %>% summarize_all(mean) %>% select(1:51)
preds <- model %>% predict(as.matrix(df[,2:51]))
hist(preds[,1])
```

As we structured our model, we will get predicted probabilities for each class. This is shown in the histogram as follows:

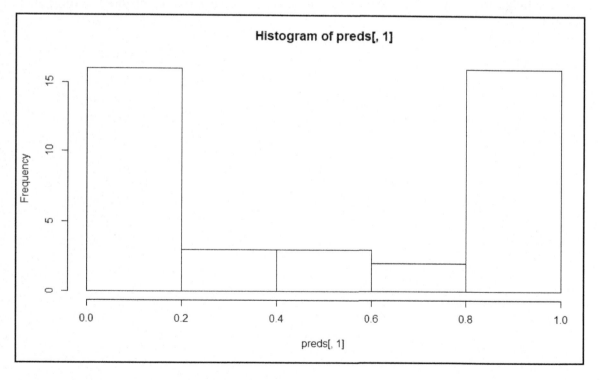

Distribution of predicted class (i.e. sentiment) probabilities

So, this is roughly the same distribution as before (recall that before we had no probabilities, but we inferred the sentiment directly). This is a good sign that the model might be doing the right things, but as always, it is better to take a look directly at the data.

Summary

In this chapter, we covered a lot! We learned how to use dense instead of sparse vectors to represent words, using word2vec or GloVe, although we only used GloVe. We worked with an annotated lexicon; tidy data can already bring a lot of insight! No need to bring in the heavy artillery in many cases. We saw that slightly more complicated models may not perform well (adding layers to the feed-forward neural network); surprisingly, much more complicated models can (using bidirectional LSTMs)! After that, we provided a reference for connecting to Twitter, while keeping in mind that terms of service should be respected. For this, we used previously calculated vector embeddings and models to evaluate the sentiment of new data. And, don't forget, a key point—always check your data! Remember, garbage in, garbage out. Even the best models will provide useless results if the wrong data is used.

Other Books You May Enjoy

If you enjoyed this book, you may be interested in these other books by Packt:

Machine Learning with R - Second Edition
Brett Lantz

ISBN: 978-1-78439-390-8

- Harness the power of R to build common machine learning algorithms with real-world data science applications
- Get to grips with R techniques to clean and prepare your data for analysis, and visualize your results
- Discover the different types of machine learning models and learn which is best to meet your data needs and solve your analysis problems
- Classify your data with Bayesian and nearest neighbor methods
- Predict values by using R to build decision trees, rules, and support vector machines
- Forecast numeric values with linear regression, and model your data with neural networks
- Evaluate and improve the performance of machine learning models
- Learn specialized machine learning techniques for text mining, social network data, big data, and more

R Deep Learning Essentials
Dr. Joshua F. Wiley

ISBN: 978-1-78528-058-0

- Set up the R package H2O to train deep learning models
- Understand the core concepts behind deep learning models
- Use Autoencoders to identify anomalous data or outliers
- Predict or classify data automatically using deep neural networks
- Build generalizable models using regularization to avoid overfitting the training data

Leave a review - let other readers know what you think

Please share your thoughts on this book with others by leaving a review on the site that you bought it from. If you purchased the book from Amazon, please leave us an honest review on this book's Amazon page. This is vital so that other potential readers can see and use your unbiased opinion to make purchasing decisions, we can understand what our customers think about our products, and our authors can see your feedback on the title that they have worked with Packt to create. It will only take a few minutes of your time, but is valuable to other potential customers, our authors, and Packt. Thank you!

Index

CPSIA information can be obtained
at www.ICGtesting.com
Printed in the USA
BVOW08s0052270218
509175BV00002B/10/P